I WILL PASS MY DRIVING TEST

I WILL PASS
MY DRIVING
TEST

MARTYN DAWES

JOHN BLAKE

Published by John Blake Publishing Ltd, 3 Bramber Court,
2 Bramber Road, London W14 9PB, England

First published in 2002

ISBN 1 904034 02 0

British Library Cataloguing-in-Publication Data: A catalogue record
for this book is available from the British Library.

Design by ENVY

Printed and bound in Great Britain by Bookmarque

1 3 5 7 9 10 8 6 4 2

Papers used by John Blake Publishing are natural, recyclable products
made from wood grown in sustainable forests. The manufacturing processes
conform to the environmental regulations of the country of origin

Contents

-- -- -- -- -- -- -- --

2: THE THEORY TEST

3: THE PRACTICAL TEST

4: USEFUL INFORMATION

Foreword

This book has been divided into four individual parts:

1: **INTRODUCTION**
2: **THE THEORY TEST**
3: **THE PRACTICAL TEST**
4: **USEFUL INFORMATION**

It is up to you to decide which part of the driving test you want to focus on now. If you are due to take your driving Theory Test, then read the Introduction and then the Theory section; if you have already passed the Theory Test and are about to take your Practical Test, then the Introduction and the Practical section are all that you need to read.

Taking your driving tests can be a traumatic and nerve-racking time. Unfortunately, because of nerves, fear, anxiety and so on, you may not be able to perform to your best ability when it counts most. The purpose of this book is to give you practical hints and tips about driving in general, the set-pieces, taking the tests, and to introduce you to an effective technique that, if applied correctly, will quite simply banish those nerves, and leave you to take your test with confidence.

Wherever you see this pen symbol ✎ you can respond to prompts by writing in the space provided.

I would like to take this opportunity to thank the owners of **www.2pass.co.uk** and **www.learners.co.uk** for their generosity in the making of this book.

Martyn Dawes

PART 1

INTRODUCTION

Emotional Freedom Technique or

HOW YOU WILL PASS YOUR DRIVING TEST

- - - - - - - - - - - - - -

Just imagine for a moment that around your body run meridians, a network for carrying electrical energy. This is the basis of acupuncture, probably the oldest recognised form of healing in the world. Meridians are not new. A cadaver approximately 5,000 years old was recently excavated from a glacier and was found to have tattoos marking relevant acupuncture points. These meridians have also been seen on cave paintings.

If you took the back off of your radio or hi-fi and poked around with a big screwdriver, the chances are that you might cause a short circuit and this might lead to loss of signal, fuzzy sound or disrupted quality.

Your body also has electrical circuits. That is how your heart beats, why we get static electricity and how we feel pain. Modern medicine actually measures electrical activity when carrying out ECGs (electro-cardiographs). When our energy stops flowing, we die. It is as simple as that; but don't take my word for it, ask your doctor.

However, these electrical circuits can also become short-circuited, and therein lies a problem.

Where Do Meridian Therapies Come From?

As mentioned above, Meridian Therapies are by no means an original concept. The classic book on acupuncture is 4,500 years old. What is surprising, I suppose, is that western physicians are only just beginning to appreciate the benefits of acupuncture, when it is clearly one of the oldest forms of medicine. Meridian Therapies cover a wide range of treatments that focus on the meridian system, a sort of channelling system for the body's energies. These include acupuncture, acupressure and a whole host of new energy therapies.

1964 saw one of the developmental jumps from acupressure to these new energy therapies when George Goodheart, a chiropractor, began to investigate links between the organs of the body, meridians and muscle strength. His research led to him developing Applied Kinesiology.

In 1979, Roger Callahan used techniques based on Applied Kinesiology on a patient named 'Mary', a water phobic, whose phobia was so severe she could not go out when it rained. The result was dramatic and instant. Mary lost her water phobia instantly! She later went for a paddle in the sea.

Roger Callahan developed this further and introduced Thought Field Therapy (TFT). This involved using individually designed sequences, or 'algorithms' of tapping on particular spots. The process required a great deal of training, skill and knowledge.

In 1995, a Stanford engineer and student of Roger Callahan's technique, Gary Craig, simplified TFT into a universally applicable protocol that he calls Emotional Freedom Technique, or EFT. This technique involved just one universal algorithm sandwiched by processes known as 'The Setup' and 'The Gamut Procedure'. Applying this simple procedure, whilst focusing on the problem at hand, has proved over and over again that it is simple, concise and yet highly effective.

How Does EFT Actually Work?

I first came across EFT whilst looking for alternative methods to alleviate pain. Somebody told me to try EFT, and that I could download the manual from Gary Craig's website. (See the **Useful Contacts and Further Information** section on page 191.) I read the manual with a healthy degree of scepticism that what was in it could change lives for the better. The claim was that, by dealing with negative emotions, long-lasting and effective change could be delivered quickly. I decided to try it, and my father was to be the guinea pig! I asked him to think of an event that he wished had never happened. He replied that being made redundant 15 years earlier still left him feeling bitter. I asked him to score that bitterness on a scale of 0 to 10 and he told me that it was a 9. After 15 years, I thought that was very high, but we all carry these sorts of thoughts around with us, every day. I guarantee that if I asked you to think of an event that still carries an emotional 'hook' for you, you could think of something that scores at least above a 7, and time, the great healer, does not always do its stuff. Sometimes it just sinks deeper into our unconscious and lurks there, waiting for the opportunity to rear its head again.

I told my father that I wanted to try out this new

technique and reluctantly he agreed ... and reluctantly I began. I say I began reluctantly because the process seemed weird, and if it did not work I would look stupid. We did one 'round' of the EFT sandwich and the score dropped to 6; then another round dropped the score to 4 and finally 0. I was astounded, and my father was astonished that the bitterness that he had carried for so long had gone.

I rang back a day later and it was still gone, and it has not returned since. I decided there and then that this was the thing for me and wanted to learn more. The next logical step was to become a qualified practitioner, which I achieved through one of the courses run by the Association of Meridian Therapists UK. (See the **Useful Contacts and Further Information** section on page 191.)

I emailed a colleague who told me that when he went to become a practitioner, he was used in front of the class as a volunteer and had burst into tears, such was the intensity of the emotion. And all of this on the first day! Hah, I thought, that would never happen to me. Well, I didn't make it to lunchtime on the first day. In a powerful example of how negative emotions can linger in the unconscious and present themselves unexpectedly, I was reduced to an absolute blubbering wreck within the first few hours! I wish to emphasise here that I am a 36-year-old man who does not cry, ever. I cannot remember ever crying, it is something I had always believed that 'real' men don't do. I was shocked, but the lesson has never been forgotten. In my private practice, I often hear clients say things like, 'I can't believe that I am telling you this,' and clients who laugh at how ridiculous the whole process seems will weep openly less than 30 seconds later when we really 'hit the point'.

EFT is an immensely powerful technique that should not be taken lightly. I give warnings in the book that must be heeded. After doing the technique for the first time, give yourself a day or two to allow your body to settle down.

I have provided a chart entitled **The Meridians, Points and How They Affect You**, which you will find on page 184. The chart will enable you to determine the direct affect that each meridian and its corresponding point will have on you physically and psychologically.

If you wish to meet a practitioner in your area, you can email me at: livelifefree@hotmail.com or call free on 0800 083 0796 to be referred to someone suitable. This is normally an answerphone service.

The Meridians

There are 12 meridians that run in pairs mirroring each other on each side of the body. In addition, there are two further meridians that flow individually.

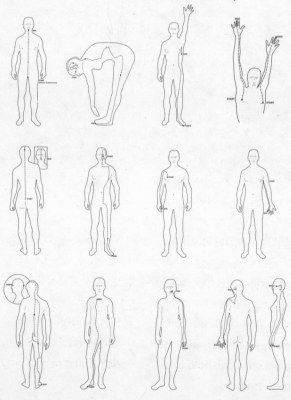

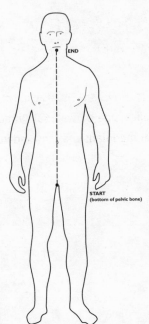

END

START
(bottom of pelvic bone)

Central Meridian

The Central Meridian runs up the front of the body in a straight line starting at the pubic bone and finishing just under the lower lip. Together with the Governing Meridian, a complete loop of the body is formed when you touch the tip of your tongue on the roof of your mouth. It is also known as the Conception Vessel and can store a large amount of energy within it. This energy can then flow into the other meridians. When blocked, it can hold past traumatic events, particularly birth trauma.

Governing Meridian

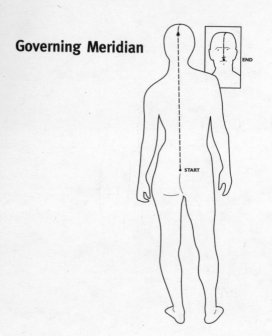

The Governing Meridian runs from the very base of the spine up the back and over the head in a straight line, coming down between the eyes and finishing just above the top lip. Together with the Central Meridian above, it forms a complete loop of the body. It is also known as a Vessel and can store large amounts of energy. Blockage may cause introvertedness and can lead to problems communicating with others. When people are stuck for something to say, they will sometimes rub the spot above the top lip inadvertently.

**Bladder
Meridian**

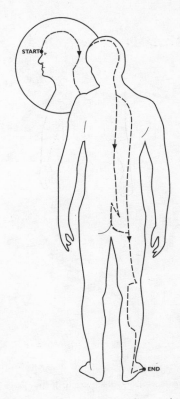

The Bladder Meridian runs from the eyebrow, up over
the head and down the middle of the back. From the
lower spine it flows down the back of the leg to the
heel, and then along the outside of the foot ending at
the little toe. It is linked with fear and courage, and
also forgetfulness and impatience.

Gall Bladder Meridian

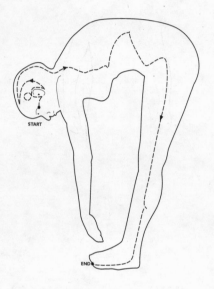

The Gall Bladder Meridian is difficult to trace, as it flows in a zigzag fashion starting at the corner of the eye and flowing down the side of the body to the fourth toe. A blockage can deplete energy but when tapped may increase determination. It aids clarity of thought but is linked with ailments such as gallstones, headaches and stiff muscles and joints.

Stomach Meridian

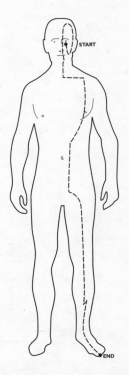

Starting from under the eye, the Stomach Meridian runs along the collarbone, down over the nipple to the groin. From here, it flows down the outside of the leg ending at the second toe. The stomach meridian is associated with indecisiveness, intuition and dogmatic thinking. As would be expected of this meridian, it can be linked with appetite disorders, indigestion, weight problems and vomiting.

Kidney Meridian

Poor decision-making, lack of willpower and a whole host of physical symptoms relate to this meridian. I find that my clients tend to like the collarbone point being tapped, and it is this meridian that flows at the collarbone point. Starting under the foot, the Kidney Meridian flows up the inside of the leg, in-between the breasts and finishes just below the collarbone.

Spleen Meridian

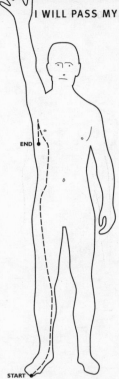

This meridian starts at the big toe and runs up the inside of the leg to the pelvis, where it goes outward from the hip and runs up through the middle of the lower rib and into the armpit. It then runs straight down the side of the body and stops at about the middle of a bra strap. It is associated with anxiety, over-eating and eating disorders. If you find that tapping under the arm is uncomfortable or unsuitable for you, you may tap the middle of the lower rib, in line with the nipple.

Lung Meridian

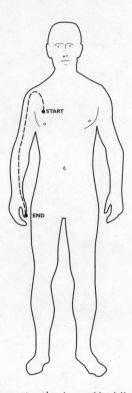

As its name suggests, the Lung Meridian is related to breathing disorders, asthma and nasal congestion. It increases positivity and is associated with intolerance and obsessive compulsive disorders. The Lung Meridian flows from just above the breast, up into the shoulder and down the arm ending at the thumb.

Large Intestine Meridian

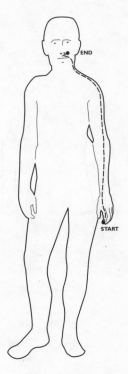

Running from the index finger, the Large Intestine Meridian flows up the edge of the arm, over the shoulder and up the side of the neck, finishing at the side of the nostril. This meridian, when blocked, may cause a harking back to the past. Guilt and wellbeing are also associated with the Large Intestine, in addition to such physical ailments as bowel problems, sinus problems and skin complaints.

Circulation Sex Meridian

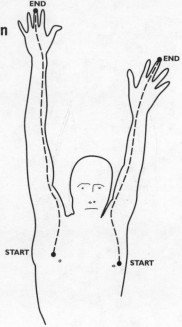

This peculiarly named meridian is often associated with low self-esteem, jealousy, regret, sexual problems and unhappiness. Physical problems related to the Circulation Sex Meridian also encompass angina, blood pressure, circulation and heart disease. Also known as the Pericardium Meridian, it flows from the outside of the breast, up the arm, ending at the tip of the middle finger.

Heart Meridian

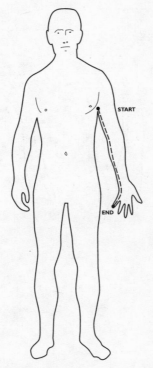

The Heart Meridian starts under the arm and runs downwards to the little finger. It is linked with compassion and joy but, when blocked, can lead to loneliness and selfishness. This meridian being so closely linked to compassion and the concept of unconditional love brings credence to the concept of the heart being the centre of love.

Small Intestine Meridian

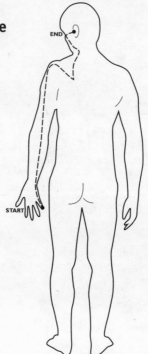

This is the meridian treated when you tap the Karate Chop point (see page 72). It removes feelings of self-doubt and lack of confidence. When blocked, this meridian can cause anxiety, bad judgement and self-hate. It runs up the back of the body starting at the tip of the little finger, up the arm, across the shoulder and ends in front of the ear.

Triple Warmer or Triple Heater Meridian

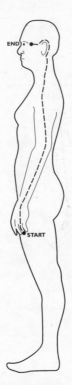

This meridian helps to move heat around the body. It is related with the inability to express emotions, loneliness and resentment. If you have problems with your bladder, allergies, fluid retention, spleen or physical pain, then this meridian may be able to help. It runs from the ring finger, up the back of the arm, across the shoulder to the neck. From here it flows around the ear, ending at the temple.

PART 2

THE THEORY TEST

Chapter 1

WHAT DO I BELIEVE?

— — — — — — — — — — — —

Taking my Theory Test is fun, easy and enjoyable.

How much do you believe that statement? Score your belief in this statement below on a scale of 0 to 10. (0 is no belief while 10 is absolute belief.)

No Belief 0 1 2 3 4 5 6 7 8 9 10 Absolute Belief

Within the pages of this section you will learn techniques to help you achieve the correct mental state for taking your Theory Test. You will also learn how to feel more relaxed and confident, and better able to deal with those last-minute nerves, as well as gain some good practical advice.

Now answer a question. Why can a sportsman – let's say a tennis player – play brilliantly for a while, and then suddenly play badly, all in the same game! The answer is in the attitude of the player. If he believes he is going to win, then he will play better; if he is confident, he will play better; if he is focused, he will play better. If he plays a succession of poor shots, the old doubts will start to set in, and his game will suffer. His play is directly affected by his mind and his thoughts; it doesn't matter how strong, fast or agile he is.

This also applies to driving tests, except that you start with all of the doubts already in your mind.

But what if we could get rid of those doubts? What if there was a technique that could not only get rid of all those doubts, but actually improve your confidence as well?

Well, there is – and this is the book to prove it!

Chapter 2

IT'S GREAT IN THEORY

Applying for the Theory Test

To get a full driving licence, you must first pass both the Practical and the Theory driving tests. To be able to take the Practical Test, you must first have sat, and passed, the Theory Test.

To book a Theory Test, you may telephone the DSA on 0870 0101 372 and pay by credit/debit card. You can also send a postal application with payment in the form of a cheque or postal order to:

DSA
PO Box 148
Salford
M5 3SY

Postal applications must be made on the relevant form

available from test centres or Approved Driving Instructors.

What do I take to the Theory Test?

- Your appointment card or booking number
- Both parts of your photocard licence
  (this must be signed), or
- Your signed driving licence and suitable photo-
  bearing identification, i.e. your passport

If you have any doubts about what identification is deemed acceptable, you may telephone the enquiry line:

UK – 0870 0101 372
NI – 01232 681831

Acceptable Photographic Identification

- A current signed passport
- Any of the listed identification cards, as long as they
  show your photograph and signature
- Workplace ID card
- Trade Union, or Students' Union card
- School bus pass
- Credit or cheque guarantee card
- Gun licence

- Proof of age card (these are issued by the Portman Group)
- A photograph of yourself, which has been signed and dated by any of the persons listed below, confirming that the photograph is a true likeness of you:
  - Minister of Religion
  - Police officer
  - Established civil servant
  - Qualified teacher
  - Solicitor
  - Doctor or medical practitioner
  - Commissioned officer in HM armed forces
  - Bank official
  - Justice of the Peace
  - Member of Parliament
  - An approved driving instructor, or DSA-certified motorcycle instructor
  - Local authority councillor
  - LGV instructor on DSA Voluntary Register of LGV Instructors

Special Needs

If you have special needs then you should mention this at the time of booking.

Help with the test is available in the following languages: Albanian, Arabic, Bengali, Cantonese,

Farsi, Gujarati, Hindi, Kurdish, Portuguese, Punjabi, Sign Language, Spanish, Tamil, Turkish, Urdu and Welsh.

If you do not speak English or any of the above languages, then you may bring an interpreter with you. This must be arranged at the time of booking. You are responsible for the fees, and the interpreter must be DSA approved.

People with dyslexia may apply to have the allotted time extended, and have the option of listening to the test through headphones.

The Theory Test

To pass this test you need to answer 30 out of 35 questions correctly. The Theory Test is conducted by means of touch-screen computers designed for ease of use. You may buy books of Theory Test questions to help you brush up on your knowledge before sitting this test, or visit the websites listed in the **Useful Contacts and Further Information** section on page 191.

Sitting the Theory Test

The questions are shown one at a time on a touch screen with the answer options displayed below. You select the answer by touching the button on the screen that corresponds to the answer you want. If you are not sure, you are able to mark the question with a flag and go back to it later. If you change your mind, you may simply touch the screen again to select a different answer.

After the Test

You should know whether you have passed in about 30 minutes. All participants are given feedback about the number of questions answered incorrectly, and any topic areas that appear problematic.

Taking the Test – Practical Tips

The first thing you should do before the Theory Test is to familiarise yourself with EFT and how it works. It will help you to overcome mental blocks that may inhibit your chances of passing, and give you techniques that really work to reduce those last-minute nerves, and make you feel more confident.

Apart from this, following the simple guidelines below will help:

• Make sure that you have a good night's sleep before the test. If you find this difficult, then try the relaxation and breathing techniques that I will explain later in the book. This will not only help you to sleep, but also help you to feel more balanced and focused.

- Wear clothes that make you feel good. Anything that helps you to get into the right frame of mind is worthwhile. Personally, when I have a major interview or exam, I always wear my best suit, as it makes me feel good, and I also treat myself to something before the event. This may be as simple as a nice coffee and a flick through a newspaper in my favourite café. Whatever it is, you are telling your mind that today is special, and that you are special, too.

- Arrive in plenty of time; it is better to be too early than too late. It will give you a chance to relax, get used to your surroundings, and perhaps to try a few of the techniques that I will explain later.

- When the test starts, read the questions carefully and answer the questions that you can do first. 'Flag' those that you cannot do; you can revisit those later.

- Be conscious of the time. The allotted time is 40 minutes; leave enough time to go through and check your answers.

- Don't try to read too much into the questions. The questions are meant to be simple, so don't complicate them.

- If you are stuck for an answer, then try a process of elimination. Identify the options that you know are wrong, and then the ones that seem unlikely. The answer that is most sensible will probably be the right one.

- If you have access to the Internet and wish to try some example questions, you will find example tests at **www.learners.co.uk** and **www.2pass.co.uk**

Chapter 3
IT'S ALL IN THE MIND

As important as preparing yourself educationally for the test is the need to prepare yourself mentally. It means overcoming all of those nagging doubts, all the little voices that are telling you that you cannot do it. You can, and here is how.

Blocks, Beliefs and Reasons

Give me one good reason why you should not pass your Theory Test. Write it below.

Now score your belief in this reason on a scale of 0 to 10 in the space below.

No Belief 0 1 2 3 4 5 6 7 8 9 10 **Absolute Belief**

The first thing I would like to tell you is that your reason is not a reason, *it is a belief*. What's more, not only is it a belief, but it is *your* belief, or your 'truth'.

If you were able to eliminate this belief, would it improve your chances of passing? You bet it would! Now have a look at the following statement again:

Taking my Theory Test is fun, easy and enjoyable.

What is stopping you from achieving this? What little nagging doubts do you have in the back of your mind? I would like you to write a list of everything that you believe is stopping you from passing your driving test. I have started you off with a few common examples, although they may not be relevant to you specifically. You should write these in the space provided below. Please do not be tempted just to skip this bit or think of them without writing them down. To get the full benefit of this book, you should participate in all of the exercises in the order shown.

My nerves affect me.

No Belief 0 1 2 3 4 5 6 7 8 9 10 **Absolute Belief**

I am not confident enough.

✎

No Belief 0 1 2 3 4 5 6 7 8 9 10 Absolute Belief

I have failed before, so why not this time?

✎

No Belief 0 1 2 3 4 5 6 7 8 9 10 Absolute Belief

My Blocks to Achieving Success in the Theory Test

[List below the reasons stopping you from passing and score your belief in each of your blocks out of 10]

....

✎

No Belief o 1 2 3 4 5 6 7 8 9 10 Absolute Belief

....

✎

No Belief o 1 2 3 4 5 6 7 8 9 10 Absolute Belief

....

✎

No Belief o 1 2 3 4 5 6 7 8 9 10 Absolute Belief

....

No Belief 0 1 2 3 4 5 6 7 8 9 10 Absolute Belief

....

No Belief 0 1 2 3 4 5 6 7 8 9 10 Absolute Belief

....

No Belief 0 1 2 3 4 5 6 7 8 9 10 Absolute Belief

These are known as 'blocks', as they block you mentally and hinder your ability to pass your test. Later, I will show you how to eliminate these blocks that may be hindering your success.

Your Unconscious Mind

Your unconscious mind is an immensely powerful tool. If you doubt this statement, then consider this: If I told you that you were worthless, dumb or stupid over a period of time, how long would it take before you were emotionally affected, before your head dropped, your self-confidence started to slip away? A year ... a month ... a week?

Your unconscious mind makes up 88% of the brain's volume and keeps our hearts beating, lungs breathing and a million other things all at once. It cannot reason or learn but accepts things at face value. It does not argue but merely obeys. It is much like a computer; you programme the information in and it does as it is told.

Think about this. Ideas, thoughts or instructions lodged in this part of the brain become fact. The unconscious mind accepts these as the absolute truth. But what if we were programming in all the wrong sort of information? Well, we do, all of the time. '*I bet I will fail my Theory Test,*' or '*my nerves will get to me,*' or even '*I am not good enough to pass.*' In fact, all of the 'beliefs' that you wrote down in the previous exercise.

If somebody calling you worthless over a long period of time may lead you to feel worthless, what if that person told you that you will fail your test, or that you are no good at tests. Even if meant as a joke, these comments can settle in the deepest recesses of your unconscious mind. When it comes to take the test, you cannot perform to your full potential, because you will fail. It has become one of your truths! It has become a barrier to passing. And you may have more barriers set deep into your belief system.

This may happen even if that person telling you that you will fail is yourself. Reflect back on the list you made earlier; these are all your beliefs, or your truths. This is what you are telling yourself.

So now we are going to find out how to banish those beliefs.

Chapter 4

USING EMOTIONAL FREEDOM TECHNIQUE

I will now show you an easy-to-use – yet remarkable – technique that can, quite simply, change your life!

This technique, which I described briefly in the Introduction, is called Emotional Freedom Technique, or EFT for short. Gary Craig developed EFT from a highly complex and lengthy therapy. He simplified it, and made it available to all. It was an extremely generous gesture once you realise the impact EFT can have on our everyday lives. Gary's website address can be found in the **Useful Contacts and Further Information** section on page 191, and I recommend it as a source of useful information and case histories.

The Discovery Statement

Gary Craig realised that 'the cause of all negative emotion is a disruption in the body's energy system'.

Your negative emotions about your Theory Test, your blocks, are caused by a disruption in the body's energy system.

Distressing Memory = Short Circuit = Negative Emotion

Straighten out the short circuit and the negative memory goes away and, with it, the illness, blocks or barriers that are inhibiting you.

Simply put, energy flows around the body like a river, but that energy can get blocked, in the same way as a log can block a river. The energy cannot continue to flow until the blockage is removed. It will either build up or take an alternate course. This can cause a 'short circuit' in the energy system that needs to be corrected.

To correct it, all you need to do is tap the meridian at a specified point while focusing on the problem.

Right now, you are probably thinking, 'Come off it, it cannot be that simple.' But I will *prove* it to you. You do not even have to believe it, it will work anyway. The technique takes 10 minutes to learn.

Your Daily Affirmation

Now is the time to choose a daily affirmation. Make no mistake; affirmations used properly are your most powerful tool to self-improvement. However, the critical factor is actually choosing a suitable affirmation. Here are a few examples:

- *Taking my Theory Test is fun, easy and enjoyable.*
- *I can take my Theory Test with confidence.*
- *I am calm and confident when taking my Theory Test.*

As the use of your affirmation will be dominant in your preparation, when choosing your affirmation you must bear three things in mind:

1: The affirmation must be in the present tense, as if you are taking your test now.

2: It must also relate to taking your test, and not passing. This is because you will not know if you pass until the end of your test, so you need to take it to pass. If you are 'calm and confident when passing your test', your unconscious mind may think that this means you will be calm and confident when you are being told that you have passed. Your unconscious mind can take things very literally!

3: You need to choose an affirmation that gets you going. One that makes you say 'Yeah' when you repeat it, one that appeals to all of your hopes, dreams and desires.

There is truth in the old saying 'Beware of what you wish for, it may just come true'.

For the purpose of this section, I will use '*Taking my Theory Test is fun, easy and enjoyable*', but you can simply substitute this for an affirmation that is more appropriate for you.

Do you remember at the beginning of the Theory Test section I asked you to score this statement?

Wouldn't it be nice to be able to increase that score? Well, that is exactly what we are going to do.

Chapter 5
THE PROCESS

At first, the steps may appear long-winded or cumbersome, but as you become acquainted with them, a complete round will only take about a minute or less.

The technique consists of four stages and is known as the EFT sandwich.

1. **The Setup**
2. **The Sequence** (bread)
3. **The Gamut Procedure** (cheese)
4. **The Sequence Repeated** (bread)

As mentioned earlier, you will need to focus in on the problem while tapping the specific points listed in **The Sequence** section. When going through this process, it is best to keep the following guidelines in mind.

- If any of the points feel nicer than others, it may be worthwhile tapping these a little longer, for as long as you want; in fact, you cannot overtap.

- If any point feels sore or really hurts, try switching to the other side of the body, or just touching the point for two breaths without tapping.

- Your body may react in different ways so do not be alarmed if something out of the ordinary happens. You may be opening meridians that have not flowed properly for some time, and that can feel strange.

- After doing this procedure for the first time, I would recommend that you give yourself two or three days before trying it again. This will give your body time to settle.

1: The Setup

To achieve success, you need to prepare your unconscious mind, and that includes neutralising blocks to healing. This is done in The Setup.

Decide which hand you would feel most comfortable tapping with – if you are right-handed, this will probably be your right hand, and vice versa.

Now look at your non-tapping hand palm upwards. Locate the edge of your hand in-between the wrist and base of your little finger. This is the point where you would 'karate chop' something if you so desired! It is therefore called the Karate Chop or KC point (see the diagram on page 72).

Remind yourself of your affirmation

Say out loud the following statements while tapping the KC point on one hand with the four fingers of the other hand.

- **'Even though it will never be possible for me to achieve my goal statement, I want to deeply and completely accept myself.'**

- 'Even if it is unsafe for me to achieve my goal statement, I want to deeply and completely accept myself.'

- 'Even if it is unsafe *for others* for me to achieve my goal statement, I want to deeply and completely accept myself.'

- 'Even though I have unique blocks stopping me from achieving my goal statement, I want to deeply and completely accept myself.'

- 'Even though I don't deserve to achieve my goal statement, I want to deeply and completely accept myself.'

As you said those statements, did any of them touch a nerve, or 'hit the spot'?

If so, write the statement here:

✎ *Even though I have unique blocks stopping me from achieving my goal statement, I want to deeply & completely accept myself*

Is there anything that you think that you ought to have said? Yes/No *yes*

If so, write it here: *I will pass my driving test*

(The Setup statement should begin '**Even though I ...**' and finish with '**... I want to deeply and completely accept myself.**')

✎ *Even though I have unique blocks stopping me from achieving my goal statement, I want to deeply & completely accept myself. I will pass my driving test*

If you have written any further statements, then say these three times each while tapping the KC point with the four fingers of the other hand.

2: The Sequence

The following diagrams show the points that you need to tap. It does not matter which side of the body you use, or indeed if you switch sides while in the middle of the sequence. Tapping should be done fairly firmly but not enough to bruise yourself! If a point hurts, instead of tapping just hold the point for two breaths. If you physically cannot tap a point, then don't worry, you could imagine tapping it or miss it out altogether. You should tap about seven times fairly quickly.

EB Eyebrow	At beginning of eyebrow at top of nose	Use the index finger and middle finger to tap this point

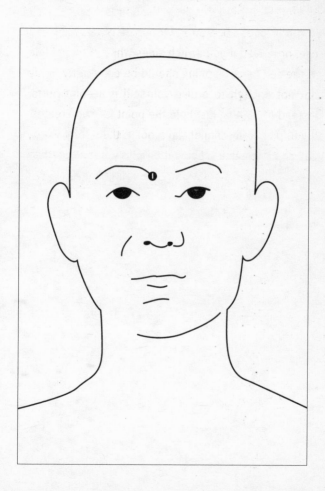

EC Eye Corner	On bone on outside corner of eye	Use the index finger and middle finger to tap this point

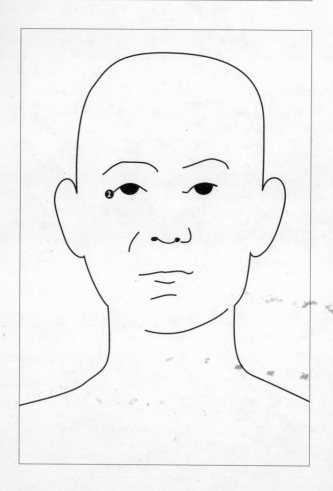

UE Under Eye	On bone just under the eye	Use the index finger and middle finger to tap this point

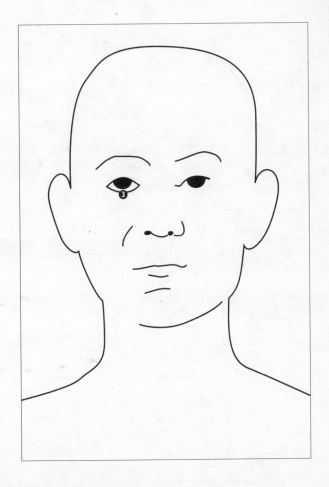

| UN Under Nose | Between nose and upper lip | Use the index finger and middle finger to tap this point |

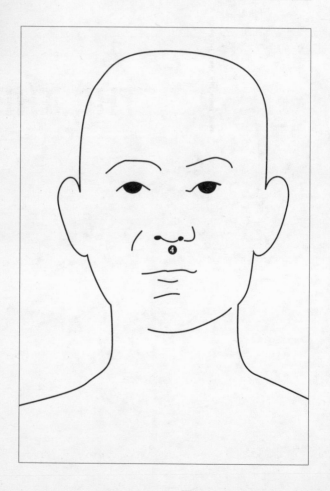

CH Chin	Centre of chin under lower lip	Use the index finger and middle finger to tap this point

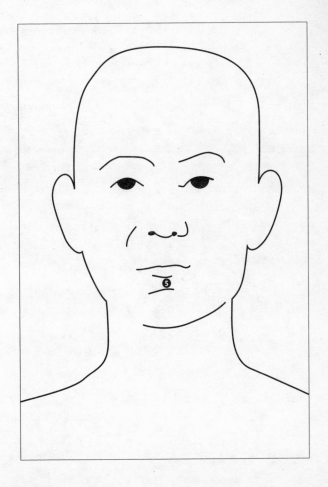

CB Collarbone	Place finger on collarbone. Move it into centre of body until you reach the corner of the collarbone	Use all four fingers to tap the corner of the collarbone hard if you can

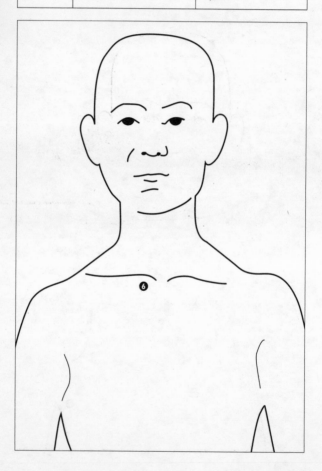

UA Under Arm	Under the arm approx. 4ins below armpit in line with the nipple	Use a flat palm to 'lightly slap' this point

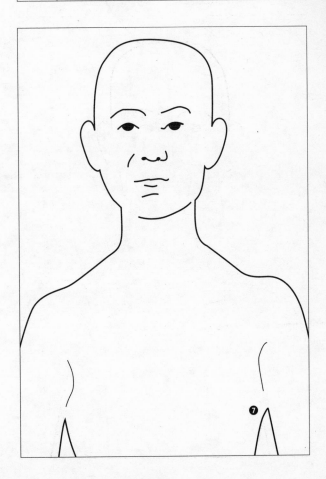

TH Thumb	Outside edge of thumb at base of nail	Use the index finger and middle finger to tap this point

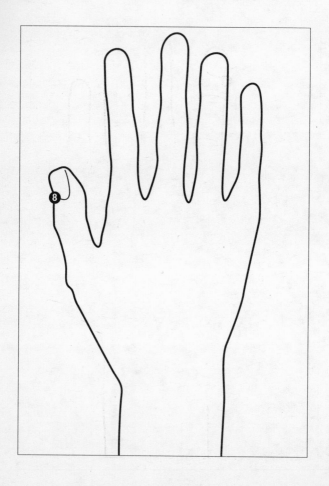

IF Index Finger	At base of nail on side facing thumb	Use the index finger and middle finger to tap this point

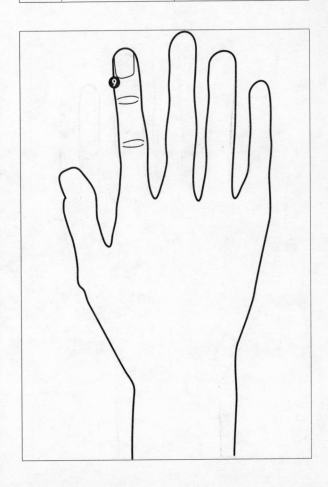

MF Middle Finger	At base of nail on side facing thumb	Use the index finger and middle finger to tap this point

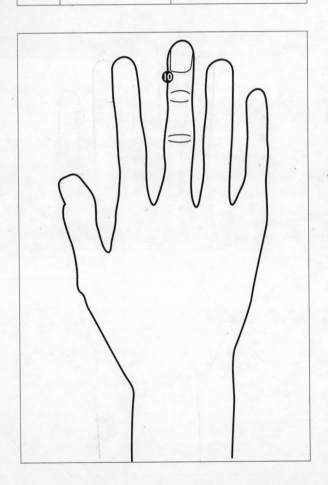

LF Little Finger	At base of nail on side facing thumb	Use the index finger and middle finger to tap this point

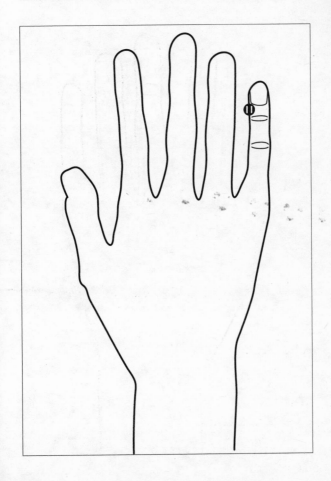

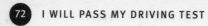

| KC Karate Chop | Outside of hand between top of wrist bone and base of little finger | Use all four fingers to tap this point |

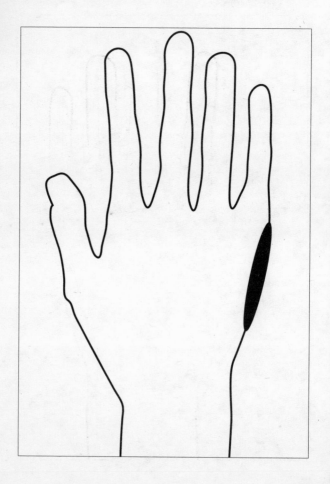

GS Gamut Spot	Back of hand, in-between ring and little finger knuckles, about 1 in back up hand	Use the index finger and middle finger to tap this point

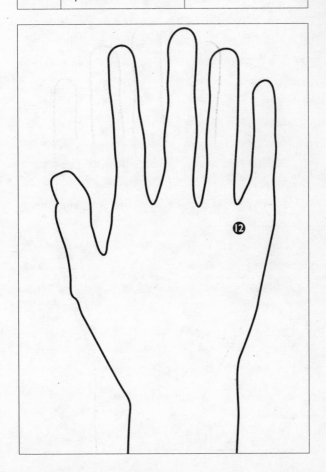

3: The Gamut Procedure

While you continually tap the Gamut Point, perform the following steps. These steps will fine tune the brain and help the brain to become more balanced. This looks probably even more strange than the earlier steps!

1. Close your eyes
2. Open your eyes
3. Look hard down left while holding your head straight
4. Look hard down right while holding your head straight
5. Roll your eyes in a **steady** circle, as if your nose was the centre of a clock
6. Roll your eyes in a **steady** circle in the opposite direction
7. Count rapidly from 1 to 5
8. Hum a few notes of a tune
9. Count rapidly for 1 to 5 again

4: The Sequence Repeated

━ ━ ━ ━ ━ ━ ━ ━ ━ ━ ━ ━ ━

Now repeat **The Sequence**, working through all the individual treatment points, from The Eyebrow to The Gamut Spot.

That is the end of this part of the technique. So how have you done? Repeat out loud your affirmation.

'Taking my Theory Test is fun, easy and enjoyable.'

Now score your belief in your ability to achieve this.

No Belief 0 1 2 3 4 5 6 7 8 9 10 Absolute Belief

Has it increased? If so, by how much?

Repeat the steps above, but you will not need to do **The Gamut Procedure** again, until you get your score as high as possible.

In the unlikely event of your score not increasing try changing rooms, and drinking water before trying again. (See the **Troubleshooting** section on page 188.)

Daily affirmation: '*Taking my Theory Test is fun, easy and enjoyable.*'

This is your daily affirmation. Make no mistake, this is one of your most useful tools to passing your Theory Test. You should start to say this every day as soon as possible. It does not matter if you believe it or not; you could use EFT to boost your belief daily, but if not, just saying it every day, whether you believe it or not, will have a powerfully positive effect on you. If you find yourself thinking 'But ... ' then you may neutralise the 'but' by using EFT.

For example, you could say to yourself, 'Taking my Theory Test is fun, easy and enjoyable,' but into your mind pops '... but you are a failure' or '... but you are not ready'. These are the thoughts to eliminate as they serve no useful purpose.

I will now show you just how to eliminate all of those negative thoughts and emotions.

Chapter 6
CLEARING THE BLOCKS

Now that your belief in your affirmation has improved, you need to start breaking down your blocks to success. These are the blocks that you listed earlier in Chapter 3.

This is done using the four stages outlined in Chapter 5.

1. **The Setup**
2. **The Sequence**
3. **The Gamut Procedure**
4. **The Sequence Repeated**

Turn back to the list of blocks that you wrote down earlier and select one to erase now. For the purpose of this exercise, I will use '*I have failed before therefore I will probably fail again*'.

Now score your belief in your statement:

✎

No Belief 0 1 2 3 4 5 6 7 8 9 10 **Absolute Belief**

Your aim now is to get the score as low as possible.

1: The Setup
Tapping the KC spot repeat:

> **'Even though *I have failed before and will probably fail again*, I want to deeply and completely accept myself.'**

Yours may be:

> **'Even though *my nerves affect me*, I want to deeply and completely accept myself.'**

or

> **'Even though *I am not confident enough*, I want to deeply and completely accept myself.'**

2: The Sequence
Now choose a reminder statement to say as you tap on each point. I am going to say '*I will probably fail again*'.

Now tap on all of the treatment points while repeating your reminder statement. Really tune into and think about your block.

Remember:

- If any of the points feel nicer than others, it may be worthwhile tapping these a little longer, for as long as you want, in fact; you cannot overtap

- If any point feels sore or really hurts, try switching to the other side of the body, or just holding the point for two breaths

- Your body may react in different ways, so do not be alarmed if something out of the ordinary happens. You may be opening meridians that have not flowed properly for some time, and that can feel strange

3: The Gamut Procedure
Now perform The Gamut Procedure as described in Chapter 5 on page 74.

4: The Sequence Repeated
Repeat the sequence.

Now score your belief in your block:

✎

No Belief 0 1 2 3 4 5 6 7 8 9 10 Absolute Belief

Has it gone down? Do the whole treatment again, *although you need not do The Gamut Procedure again*, until you get your score as low as you possibly can.

> **Now repeat this process for each of your blocks. I realise that this may take a little time, but you are eradicating a lifetime's worth of blocks and replacing them with one – your affirmation.**

If, like many of us, you have a great long list that keeps growing as you identify more blocks, then just do two, three or as many as you can cope with, each day. You will notice that as you eradicate them one by one, you will start to feel better in yourself, your confidence may improve and you may begin to feel more relaxed.

When you are happy that you have cleared these blocks, then please proceed.

Finding a Booster Spot

It would be very useful if you could identify one or two specific points that really work for you. This would be an important find, as it may provide a shortcut for you; instead of tapping all of the points in sequence, just tap the ones that make a difference. This will cut out all of the other stages.

When you are in a stressful situation and want to relax, if you have found a booster spot that helps you relax, then that is all you will need to tap. In fact, if you are in a public place and you wish to be discreet, you will not even have to tap; you can just touch the point while you are breathing. All you need to do is think of a problem, give it a name for your reminder statement, score it, and then just tap your booster spot.

When going through **The Sequence**, are there any particular points that feel really nice for you? Why not try scoring your belief after each point and seeing if any has a positive effect on your score? A booster spot may be specific to a particular problem; for instance, a spot that helps you to relax may be different from one that increases your confidence. It is just a matter of finding the ones that work for you.

Chapter 7

VISUALISATION – TAKING THE TEST IN YOUR MIND

You may well want to forget it, but your test will not go away! An effective tool available for your use at any time is to take the test in your mind. This will work for both the Practical and Theory Tests. This is not as weird as it may sound. If you doubt the effectiveness of this exercise, cast your mind back to the earlier chapter when I explained about the unconscious mind. It does not reason or think, it just obeys. More importantly, it cannot tell the difference between you visualising or imagining something and reality. The more real it seems in your mind, the more effective it will be.

In your mind, go into the waiting room and sit down. It does not matter if you have never been in there; just imagine what it may be like. What does it feel like? Are you nervous, anxious ... are you getting any feeling at all?

I would imagine that most of us would be nervous. If just thinking about it does not raise any emotion, but you know that it will be there on the day, then try again, but really try to imagine it. What does the room look like in your mind, what does it smell like, is there a pile of magazines on the table? Imagine your name being called out and you have to go forward to take the test. You are now in front of the touch screen about to commence the test. Now score the feeling from 0 to 10 on the scale below.

No Feeling 0 1 2 3 4 5 6 7 8 9 10 Extreme Feeling

Give it a name – *nervousness*, *anxiety*, etc. (This will be your reminder statement.)

Now do the technique to neutralise that feeling, while thinking about the situation. You will need to treat each emotion separately. Do as many rounds as it takes to bring the emotional intensity down to as low a score as possible.

Your statement may be:

'Even though I am nervous when taking my test, I deeply and completely accept myself.'

Now imagine going into the Theory Test room and commencing the Theory Test. As you go through it in your mind, as soon as you start to feel any emotional content from each situation then perform the following steps:

- Score the feeling
- Give it a name (this will be your reminder statement)
- Now use EFT to neutralise the feeling

Rerun the situation in your mind; if there is no emotional content, then you can proceed with your Theory Test.

Take the whole test in your mind. Treat the emotional content of each situation using the four steps above. When you can take the test competently in your mind, then you are a significant step closer to passing.

Make no mistake about it. Using the visualisation technique will significantly improve your chances of passing if performed correctly.

Specific Blocks

For many of us, one particular part of the test will cause the most problems, the most nerves and a greater chance of not passing.

Why not use EFT to help with that specific situation?

Let's use an example:
'*I hate computers.*'

Use EFT to overcome this and move on to any other specific fears.

Score how much you hate computers. (0 would be no hate, while 10 would be absolute hatred.) Follow the simple steps, and why not look for a booster spot?

Start off with **The Setup**: '*Even though I hate computers, I deeply and completely accept myself.*'

Next, do The Sequence, your reminder statement could be simply '*I hate computers,*' while you think about sitting the test and how much you hate computers.

Next do **The Gamut Procedure**.

Now do **The Sequence Repeated**.

Now score I hate computers. Has it gone down? It should have. If not, see the **Troubleshooting** section on page 188.

Now repeat the process until you get the score as low as possible; you should be able to get it down to a o or 1. You need not perform **The Gamut Procedure** again.

Perform these stages for any specific problems, fears or anxieties that you have.

Confidence Booster

Score your belief that you will pass your Theory Test. You can also use EFT to help increase your confidence.

Let's use '*I will pass my Theory Test.*'

No Belief 0 1 2 3 4 5 6 7 8 9 10 Absolute Belief

What is your score? If it is low then you can perform the four stages of EFT to help in this area. Follow the simple steps; it would be extremely beneficial to find a booster spot for this exercise, and I have written out the steps below with this in mind. Remember, you are looking for individual points that substantially increase your score, or perhaps just feel different.

Start off with **The Setup**: '*Even though I don't believe that I can pass my Theory Test, I deeply and completely accept myself.*' Now score the statement.

✎

No Belief 0 1 2 3 4 5 6 7 8 9 10 Absolute Belief

Next, do **The Sequence**. Your reminder statement could be simply '*I don't believe*', while you think about sitting the test and how much you don't believe that you can pass. **After you tap each individual point, score your statement.**

✎

Next do **The Gamut Procedure**.

Now do **The Sequence Repeated**.

Score the statement again. Try just tapping the booster spot while repeating '*disbelief*', and see if it makes a difference. If not, you have got the wrong spot, or you need to do the complete procedure again.

Now score '*I believe that I can pass my Theory Test.*' Has it gone up? It should have. If not, see the **Troubleshooting** section on page 188.

Relaxation

You may also benefit from two techniques for
relaxation. The first one is possibly the most effective
relaxation technique that I know. It works really well,
especially if you are very stressed. Here is what you
do:

Method 1

- Sit comfortably (you may lie down if you wish, but I
  find sitting is the best position)
- Cross your legs
- Cross your arms over in the opposite direction. Let
  them rest loosely in your lap
- Breathe in through your nose with the tip of your
  tongue on the roof of your mouth (this is to connect
  two meridians – the Central Meridian and the
  Governing Meridian)
- Breathe out through your mouth with your tongue
  down flat. As you exhale, repeat 'balance'
- As you exhale and repeat 'balance', let your body
  relax further with each breath. Personally, I
  concentrate on letting my shoulders relax and the
  rest of my body seems to follow
- Do this for two minutes

Note: This is a powerful technique so do not overdo it, especially if you are about to drive or operate heavy machinery.

Method 2

If you are feeling especially tense, then EFT is a useful tool. I have written it down below, again with the intention of finding a booster spot. If you have already found a booster spot, then just try tapping that point alone while repeating '*tension*'. If this does not work, then you will have to find another booster spot for '*tension*' or go through the complete procedure:

- Score how tense you feel (0 being completely relaxed while 10 is very tense)
- Start off with **The Setup**. '*Even though I am tense, I deeply and completely accept myself*'
- Now score the statement

Next, do **The Sequence**. Your reminder statement could be simply 'this tension', while you think about sitting the test and how much you don't believe that you can pass. After you tap each individual point, score your statement.

Next do **The Gamut Procedure**.

Now do **The Sequence Repeated**.

Score the statement again. Try just tapping the booster spot while repeating 'this tension', and see if it makes a difference. If not, you have got the wrong spot, or you need to do the complete procedure again.

On the Day

So the day of your Theory Test is here. From the very moment you wake up, you should be thinking, 'Taking my Theory Test is fun, easy and enjoyable,' or your chosen affirmation.

Use EFT to eliminate any last-minute worries and nerves. Practise the relaxation technique, and do not allow any negative thoughts about passing your Theory Test to pop into your head. If they do, simply dismiss them and replace with your affirmation.

Dress to feel good. Wear clothes that make you feel special.

Arrive in good time.

When waiting, use the booster spot if necessary. As I mentioned before, all you need to do is hold the point concerned. You may also practise the relaxation technique unobtrusively in the waiting room. Believe me, I have done it, and people are normally too wrapped up in their own concerns to worry about you. If you wish to do a last-minute round of EFT, then perhaps you could dash to the loo!

If you feel that you would like to try other simple and discreet methods of controlling your nerves, providing you with more focus, or a feeling of confidence and control, refer to the Breathing Exercises section on page 178. You will find three different exercises which can be practised well in advance of your tests, and then you can use them just before the test itself to provide you with an extra tool to achieve success.

It may also be useful to remind yourself of the practical advice provided in the Practical Tips section in Chapter 2.

Good luck!

PART 3

THE PRACTICAL TEST

- -

Chapter 1

WHAT DO I BELIEVE?

I am relaxed and confident when taking my Practical Driving Test.

How much do you believe that statement? Score your belief in this statement below on a scale of 0 to 10. (0 is no belief while 10 is absolute belief.)

No Belief 0 1 2 3 4 5 6 7 8 9 10 Absolute Belief

Within the pages of this section you will learn techniques to help you achieve the correct mental state for taking your Practical Test. You will also learn how to feel more relaxed and confident, and better able to deal with those last-minute nerves, as well as gain some good practical advice.

Now answer a question. Why can a sportsman – let's

say a tennis player – play brilliantly for a while, and then suddenly play badly, all in the same game! The answer is in the attitude of the player. If he believes he is going to win, then he will play better; if he is confident, he will play better; if he is focused, he will play better. If he plays a succession of poor shots, the old doubts will start to set in, and his game will suffer. His play is directly affected by his mind and his thoughts; it doesn't matter how strong, fast or agile he is.

This also applies to driving tests, except that you start with all of the doubts already in your mind.

But what if we could get rid of those doubts? What if there was a technique that could not only get rid of all doubts, but actually improve your confidence as well?

Well, there is – and this is the book to prove it!

Chapter 2

PUTTING IT ALL INTO PRACTICE

Before you can learn to drive, you must be in receipt of a provisional driving licence. This can be obtained by filling in form DI, available at any post office, and sending it off. Once the licence has been sent to you, you must sign it on the back before it becomes valid.

You may only drive once you have reached the age of 17, and then only if accompanied by somebody over 21. A person who is registered disabled, or receives a mobility allowance, may drive at the minimum age of 16.

Before getting into the car for the first time, ensure that you are insured to drive the vehicle, and that the vehicle is taxed, and has a current MOT. You must also display L-plates on the front and rear of the vehicle.

To obtain a full driving licence, you must first pass both the Practical and the Theory driving tests. To be able to take the Practical Test, you must first have sat, and passed, the Theory Test.

The easiest way to book your Practical driving test is to telephone the DSA on 0870 0101 372 and pay by credit/debit card. You will need to be able to provide the following information:

- Your driver number (you will find this on your licence)
- Name, address and telephone number
- Your Theory Test certificate number
- Your Driving School code number (if known)
- Your preferred dates and any unacceptable dates
- Whether you can take a test at short notice
- Any special circumstances or disabilities
- Your credit/debit card details
- The type of test required

Cancellations

You must give at least 10 full working days' notice; this does not include the day you made your booking or the day of the test. If you fail to do so, you will lose your fee.

Disabilities

The DSA will accommodate you no matter how severe your disability; you will still be able to take the same test. More time will be allowed for you to take your test in order that the examiner can discuss your disability and any special adaptations that are made to your vehicle.

What Do I Take to the Practical Test?

- Your Theory Test pass certificate
- Both parts of your photocard licence, or your provisional licence (this must be signed)
- Suitable photo-bearing identification (i.e. passport)

If you have any doubts about what identification is deemed acceptable, you may telephone the enquiry line:

UK – 0870 0101 372

NI – 01232 681831

Acceptable Photographic Identification

- A current signed passport
- Any of the listed identification cards, as long as they show your photograph and signature
- Workplace ID card

- Trade Union, or Students' Union card
- School bus pass
- Credit or cheque guarantee card
- Gun licence
- Proof of age card (these are issued by the Portman Group)
- A photograph of yourself, which has been signed and dated by any of the persons listed below, confirming that the photograph is a true likeness of you:
  - Minister of Religion
  - Police officer
  - Established civil servant
  - Qualified teacher
  - Solicitor
  - Doctor or medical practitioner
  - Commissioned officer in HM armed forces
  - Bank official
  - Justice of the Peace
  - Member of Parliament
  - An approved driving instructor, or DSA-certified motorcycle instructor
  - Local authority councillor
  - LGV instructor on DSA Voluntary Register of LGV Instructors

Special Needs

If you have special needs then you should mention this at the time of booking.

If you do not speak English, then you may bring an interpreter with you. This must be arranged at the time of booking. The interpreter must be over 16, not an Approved Driving Instructor, and must wear a seatbelt for the duration of the test.

Pre-test Preparation

You should have had adequate tuition with a qualified driving instructor before attempting to take your Practical Test. To find an instructor, the best way is normally by word of mouth, however, the local paper normally has adverts or you could use a website such as **www.learners.co.uk** which has a National Directory of Driving Tuition to enable you to find driving schools in your area. This facility will also help you look for specific requests, such as disabled facilities.

As well as reading books such as this, there is plenty of information on the Internet. In addition to **www.learners.co.uk** you should also look at **www.2pass.co.uk** Both of these sites are interesting and informative. **www.driving-tests.co.uk** is the website address for the Driving Standards Agency. This site has a lot of specific information regarding special needs, and lists any recent changes to the test.

The Practical Test

The Practical Test is designed to allow you to demonstrate that you can drive safely unaccompanied. It does not mean that you are an expert driver with little more to learn. You should have had plenty of practice on all kinds of roads, in as many conditions as you can. You will be required to carry out any two of the following set-pieces:

• Reversing around a corner
• Turning in the road
• Reverse parking
• Parallel parking

You may also be asked to carry out the emergency stop procedure. This is currently requested at random in about a third of all tests.

All of the above procedures, plus practical hints and tips, are outlined in the following pages.

Chapter 3
THE DAY OF THE TEST

- - - - - - - - - - - - - - - -

You will meet the examiner at the test centre and will need to have the documents listed earlier. You will also be asked to sign and read an insurance declaration. Make sure that your insurance is valid before you take the test.

You will then be asked to accompany the examiner outside; they may engage you in a little conversation to help you relax.

You will be asked to read a vehicle number plate. If you have any doubts about your eyesight, then you should have your eyes tested by an optician. If you struggle to read the number plate, the examiner will measure out the exact distance of 20.5 metres. If you still cannot read the number plate, the test will end and you will lose your fee.

The examiner will then ask you to get into your car and make yourself comfortable.

Basic Routines and Skills

These are recognised procedures for completing the
necessary set pieces, however, your instructor may
have a slightly different approach. You should always
adhere to the routine shown to you by your instructor
if different to those shown in this book.

1: COCKPIT DRILL

You should learn this drill and carry it out before you
start on any journey, however short. Always remember
that you are responsible for the safety of your
passengers.

- Doors – Ensure that your door and the doors of all
  passengers are securely shut.
- Seat – Adjust your seat for comfort and practicality.
  You should be able to depress the clutch pedal
  down to the floor without stretching.
- Steering – Your seat position should also allow
  comfortable steering. Some cars will allow you to
  adjust your steering wheel as necessary. You
  should be able to allow all pedals to gain their full
  height without your knee touching the underside of
  the steering wheel.

- Seatbelts – Ensure that all seatbelts are correctly fastened and are in working order. It is the driver's responsibility to ensure that all children under 14 have their seatbelt fastened. It is a legal requirement for all passengers to wear a seatbelt, where provided, unless they have an exemption certificate.
- Mirrors – Adjust your rear-view and wing mirrors. You should be able to see clearly in the mirror with a minimum of head movement. Your wing mirrors should be adjusted to reduce blind spots.

2: STEERING

With your hands positioned on the steering wheel at about 10 minutes to 2, fold your palms over the rim and rest your thumbs lightly upon the wheel. Keep your arms free of your body.

To steer accurately, you should look well ahead of you.

You must be able to operate your controls without looking at them. Looking down may cause your car to weave from side to side. Try to keep both of your hands on the wheel as much as possible, and always when braking or cornering.

However, there may be times when you will need to change gears, operate lights, wipers or other controls. You should practise in a safe area to ensure that you are familiar with all of the controls.

When approaching right-hand bends, move your hand to the top of the wheel ready to steer to the right around the curve of the road. Your hand should always stay in the grey area pictured (opposite, above).

When approaching left-hand bends, move your hand to the top of the wheel ready to steer to the left around the curve of the road. Your hand should always stay in the grey area pictured below.

When turning, try not to cross your hands over each other.

When turning left, you should try and stay about a metre out from the kerb. Too close and your rear wheel may roll over the kerb, or damage it through impact. You may also be forced to swing out into the path of oncoming traffic.

3: THE HILL START – UPHILL

Moving off on a gradient requires a greater degree of co-ordination involving the handbrake, clutch and accelerator pedals. Without this you may roll backwards and fail your test. The normal routine for moving away from the kerb applies.

Mirror – signal – manoeuvre. Select first gear, bring the clutch to the 'biting point' and apply higher revs than you would normally use to pull away on a level road.

Check your mirrors and look over your right shoulder. Also check to ensure that no pedestrians are crossing immediately behind the car.

If a signal is needed, then give it. When it is safe to move off, release your handbrake, and let your clutch 'bite' a little more. You should be able to feel the car pulling away slightly. Release the clutch slowly and apply a little more acceleration as the car starts to move off and gather speed.

It is worth remembering that it will be harder for your car to go uphill in the same way that it is harder for you to walk uphill. Therefore, you must build up more momentum than usual in first gear before changing. Do not fumble your next gear change as momentum will be lost.

If you have used your indicator, cancel it and drive as you would normally.

4: THE HILL START – DOWNHILL

The approved method for a downhill start is to use the footbrake to hold the car during take-up of the clutch.

Select first gear (second gear is permissible if the gradient is very steep). With the clutch pedal fully depressed, apply the footbrake.

Keeping both pedals depressed, do your visual checks to ensure that it is safe for you to move off. Do not forget to look over your shoulder.

If it is safe, release the handbrake and find the biting point with the clutch pedal. Now slowly release the footbrake.

As the car begins to move, fully release the clutch and transfer your right foot from the footbrake to the accelerator.

A steep downhill gradient may require you to stay in second gear. However, third gear is likely to be the highest gear that you will need to maintain effective control of your vehicle.

5: THE EMERGENCY STOP

This manoeuvre will be tested at random in about a third of all tests. The examiner will ask you to stop at various places during your driving test. You should always do so in a safe place. The examiner will not try to trick you into stopping in an illegal place; it is your responsibility, though, to ensure that you select a safe position for normal stops. During one of these 'stops', the examiner may tell you that, very shortly, he will ask you to stop the vehicle as if in an emergency. He will show you a signal that he will use when he requires you to carry out this procedure. This will normally be by holding up his right hand and saying 'Stop'.

This is the one occasion when you do not use the mirror-signal-manoeuvre sequence. The examiner will have checked that it is safe for you to carry out this procedure, and will not ask you to stop if it is unsafe for you to do so.

When you get the signal, release the accelerator pedal and slide your right foot on to the brake pedal. Apply firm pressure; try to judge the pedal movement so that the brakes are on the point of locking.

Hold the pedal still and, as the car slows down, gradually release the pressure. Hold the steering wheel with two hands throughout and hold the car in a straight line. Be alert for any signs of the wheels locking up.

If a skid has started, ease the footbrake, although not completely, and re-apply pressure.

Try to avoid depressing the clutch until just before you stop. This will give your car extra braking from the engine.

With the car at a standstill, and the clutch and footbrake pedals depressed, apply the handbrake and move the gear lever into neutral.

Move off again only when you have been told to do so. Do not forget the mirror-signal-manoeuvre routine. You may have stopped in the middle of the road, so look over your left shoulder as well.

The Set-Pieces

1: THE TURN IN THE ROAD

Choose a safe place with good visibility, no obstructions in the road or on the pavement (watch out for lamp posts, post boxes, telephone poles, etc.) and where you have plenty of room. Stop on the left and check that the indicator has been cancelled. Make sure the road is clear ahead of you and behind you, and check the blind spot over your right shoulder.

Engage first gear and move slowly forward using clutch control, turning your steering wheel briskly to the right. Aim to get your car at right angles across the road.

When the front of the car is about 1 metre from the kerb, and still moving slowly, start turning the steering wheel briskly to the left. As the front wheels near the kerb, depress the clutch and use your footbrake to stop. Apply the handbrake.

Select reverse gear and find the biting point. Make sure that the way is clear, check in all directions and, if clear, release the handbrake and reverse slowly across the road, turning the steering wheel as far to the left as it will go.

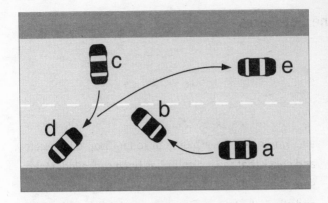

As the rear of the car nears the kerb, turn the steering wheel briskly to the right so that, when you stop, you will be nearly on a right-hand lock, ready to drive forward again. Stop before you hit the kerb, apply the handbrake and select first gear.

Make sure that the way is clear in all directions and drive forward, steering the car to the right.

You should now be able to straighten up on the left-hand side of the road.

2: REVERSE AROUND A CORNER

On the approach, draw up to the kerb on the left before the junction and cancel your indicator. Note any obstructions and the type of corner. The illustration shows a sharp turn, whereas you may have a wide, sweeping corner. Move off remembering your mirror-signal-manoeuvre sequence, and remember to check over your right-hand shoulder. Do you need to indicate? Drive to a point beyond the junction shown as point b.

Draw up about 0.5 metres from the kerb and two car lengths from the junction. If you have used your indicator, ensure that you have cancelled it. Remove your seatbelt now if you will find the procedure easier without it. Remember to put it back on afterwards. Visually check all around and, when you are ready, engage reverse gear and move off very slowly, without using any signals.

As you look through the rear window, you will see the kerb disappear, and gradually appear in the rear left-hand window. At this point, turn the steering wheel to the left. The front of the car will swing out so it is important that you check for traffic both ways, and for pedestrians behind you. Continue very slowly if clear. If a car approaches from the road you are reversing into, STOP. If the vehicle passes you and continues on its journey, you may carry on with your manoeuvre. If it stops behind you, then you are causing an obstruction. You will have to engage first gear (remember your seat-belt) and move back to point b where you can start the process again.

Straighten up when looking out of your rear window, checking that the car is running parallel to the kerb. Watch in front as well. If someone comes around the corner, then STOP. Continue when they have passed. Stop on your examiner's instruction.

3: PARALLEL PARKING

Engage the handbrake and neutral gear. Put your seatbelt back on and await your next instruction

Drive forward and stop parallel to – but not more than 1 metre away from – the car you are to park behind. Select reverse gear. Look to ensure that it is clear before you move off. Drive back very slowly and watch for the corner of the car alongside you appearing in the side window.

When you can see the corner of the car, turn the wheel to the left one full turn. Check the road in both directions and, if it is safe, continue reversing until the

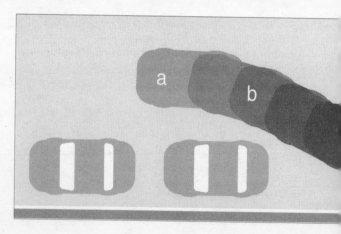

front of your car is in line with the rear of the car you are going to park behind. Turn the wheel fully to the right, ensuring that you clear the rear of the car in front. Your car will swing in towards the kerb.

You will be very close to both the kerb and the car in front. Move the car very slowly and reduce some of the right lock to ensure that the front of your car does not swing in too far. Check the distance from the kerb and the car ahead.

Once at point d, you will be close to the kerb. If you need to correct your position, you may move backwards and forwards until you are happy. Do not overdo it, though.

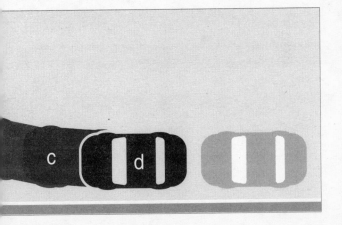

4: REVERSE PARKING – PARKING IN A BAY

- Look at the layout markings and the size of the space
- Use your mirrors and signal as necessary
- Check your position and proceed slowly
- Keep a sharp lookout all around, and watch out for pedestrians
- Park as neatly as possible with your wheels straight
- Try to ensure that you are parked neatly and evenly
- Show consideration for other road users, keep control of the vehicle and use good, effective observation

Watch These Danger Areas

Scenario a shows an approach to reverse into a bay from the right. You will be able to see the bay clearly over your right shoulder.

Scenario b shows how to approach a bay to get a clear view in your rear window. This is normally the easier option but needs plenty of space in front of the bay.

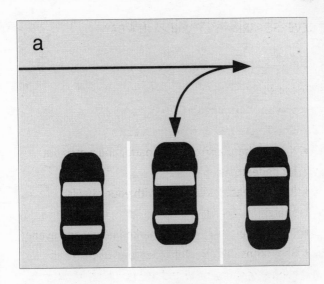

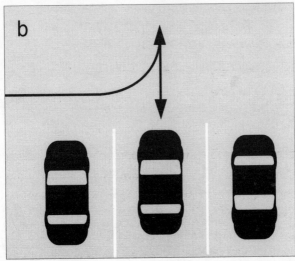

Taking the Test – Practical Tips

The first thing you should do before the Practical Test is to familiarise yourself with EFT and how it works. It will help you to overcome mental blocks that may inhibit your chances of passing, and give you techniques that really work to reduce those last-minute nerves, and make you feel more confident.

Apart from this, following the simple guidelines below will help:

• Make sure that you have a good night's sleep before the test. If you find this difficult, then try the relaxation and breathing techniques that I will explain later in the book. This will not only help you to sleep, but also help you to feel more balanced and focused.

• Wear clothes that make you feel good. Anything that helps you to get into the right frame of mind is worthwhile. Personally, when I have a major interview or exam, I always wear my best suit, as it makes me feel good, and I also treat myself to something before the event. This may be as simple as a nice coffee and a flick through a newspaper in my favourite café. Whatever it is, you are telling your mind that today is special, and that you are special, too.

- Arrive at the test centre in plenty of time, give yourself time to relax and get used to your surroundings. Use the booster spot if necessary, a technique which will be explained later.

- Listen to the instructions from your examiner carefully. Ask him to repeat them if necessary.

- Drive smoothly. Show the examiner that you deserve to have your L-plates removed.

- Maintain your best standard to the very end of the test. You could still fail right up until the end!

- If you are unsure about your eyesight, arrange a visit to an optician before the test. You must be able to read a number plate with letters approx 80mm high from a distance of 20.5 metres. If you need glasses or contact lenses to read the number plate, then these must be worn throughout the test.

Before starting the engine:

- Check that your mirrors are correctly positioned
- Make sure all doors are closed properly
- Fasten your seatbelt. Make sure that you are comfortable, and your head restraint is in its proper position
- Make sure that your handbrake is on, and you are in a neutral gear
- Remember – **mirror-signal-manoeuvre**, and don't forget to check the blind spot

After The Test

You should know whether you have passed straight away. If you have not passed, this will be because you have not reached the required standard. Your examiner will give you a report form identifying those aspects of your driving which were not acceptable. There is no 'quota' of passes.

The most common reasons for failing are:

- Taking your test too soon, with insufficient driving experience
- Driving differently from your normal practice (e.g. slower or faster)
- Loss of concentration, leading to driving errors
- Impairment of decision-making abilities, leading to poor judgement
- Inadequate skills due to poor tuition

All of these reasons can be overcome.

Chapter 4
IT'S ALL IN THE MIND

‑ ‑ ‑ ‑ ‑ ‑ ‑ ‑ ‑ ‑ ‑ ‑ ‑ ‑ ‑ ‑

As important as preparing yourself educationally for the test is the need to prepare yourself mentally. It means overcoming all of those nagging doubts, all the little voices that are telling you that you cannot do it. You can, and here is how.

Blocks, Beliefs and Reasons

Give me one good reason why you should not pass your Practical Test. Write it below.

 Can't do Manouvres

Now score your belief in this reason on a scale of 0 to 10 in the space below.

No Belief 0 1 2 3 4 5 6 7 8 9 10 **Absolute Belief**

The first thing I would like to tell you is that your reason is not a reason, it is a belief. What's more, not only is it a belief, but it is your belief, or *your* 'truth'.

If you were able to eliminate this belief, would it improve your chances of passing? You bet it would! Now have a look at the following statement again: *'I am relaxed and confident when taking my Practical Test.'*

What is stopping you from achieving this? What little nagging doubts do you have in the back of your mind? I would like you to write a list of everything that you believe is stopping you from passing your driving test. I have started you off with a few common examples, although they may not be relevant to you specifically. You should write these in the space provided below. Please do not be tempted just to skip this bit or think of them without writing them down. To get the full benefit of this book, you should participate in all of the exercises in the order shown.

My nerves affect me.

✎ No self belief that I can do the manouvres correctly

No Belief 0 1 2 3 4 5 6 7 8 9 10 **Absolute Belief**

I am not confident enough. when do t for

✎ *maiovenes*

No Belief 0 ①2 3 4 5 6 7 8 9 10 **Absolute Belief**

I have failed before, so why not this time?

✎ *Exactly*

No Belief ⓪ 1 2 3 4 5 6 7 8 9 10 **Absolute Belief**

I am a poor judge of speed/distance/etc.

✎

No Belief 0 1 2 3 4 5 6 7 ⑧ 9 10 **Absolute Belief**

My Blocks to Achieving Sucess in the Practical Test

[List below the reasons stopping you from passing]

Not Confident
when doing the
manouvres

No Belief 0 1 2 3 4 5 6 7 8 9 10 **Absolute Belief**

Nerves

No Belief 0 1 2 3 4 5 6 7 8 9 10 **Absolute Belief**

No Belief 0 1 2 3 4 5 6 7 8 9 10 **Absolute Belief**

....

✎

No Belief 0 1 2 3 4 5 6 7 8 9 10 Absolute Belief

....

✎

No Belief 0 1 2 3 4 5 6 7 8 9 10 Absolute Belief

....

✎

No Belief 0 1 2 3 4 5 6 7 8 9 10 Absolute Belief

These are known as 'blocks', as they block you mentally and hinder your ability to pass your test. I would like you to score your belief in each of your blocks out of ten. Later, I will show you how to eliminate these blocks that may be hindering your success.

Your Unconscious Mind

Your unconscious mind is an immensely powerful tool. If you doubt this statement, then consider this: If I told you that you were worthless, dumb or stupid over a period of time, how long would it take before you were emotionally affected, before your head dropped, your self-confidence started to slip away? A year ... a month ... a week?

Your unconscious mind makes up 88% of the brain's volume and keeps our hearts beating, lungs breathing and a million other things all at once. It cannot reason or learn but accepts things at face value. It does not argue but merely obeys. It is much like a computer; you programme the information in and it does as it is told.

Think about this. Ideas, thoughts or instructions lodged in this part of the brain become fact. The unconscious mind accepts these as the absolute truth. But what if we were programming in all the wrong sort of information? Well, we do, all of the time. *'I bet I will fail my driving test,'* or *'my nerves will get to me,'* or even 'I am not good enough to pass.' In fact, all of the 'beliefs' that you wrote down in the previous exercise.

If somebody calling you worthless over a long period of time may lead you to feel worthless, what if that person told you that you will fail your test, or that you are no good at tests. Even if meant as a joke, these comments can settle in the deepest recesses of your unconscious mind. When it comes to take the test, you cannot perform to your full potential, because you will fail. It has become one of your truths! It has become a barrier to passing. And you may have more barriers set deep into your belief system.

This may happen even if that person telling you that you will fail is yourself. Reflect back on the list you made earlier; these are all your beliefs, or your truths. This is what you are telling yourself.

So now we are going to find out how to banish those beliefs.

Chapter 5

USING EMOTIONAL FREEDOM TECHNIQUE

I will now show you an easy-to-use – yet remarkable – technique that can, quite simply, change your life!

This technique, which I described briefly in the Introduction, is called Emotional Freedom Technique, or EFT for short. Gary Craig developed EFT from a highly complex and lengthy therapy. He simplified it, and made it available to all. It was an extremely generous gesture once you realise the impact EFT can have on our everyday lives. Garys' website address can be found in the **Useful Contacts and Further Information** section on page 191, and I recommend it as a source of useful information and case histories.

The Discovery Statement

Gary Craig realised that 'the cause of all negative emotion is a disruption in the body's energy system'.

Your negative emotions about your Practical Test, your blocks, are caused by a disruption in the body's energy system.

Distressing Memory = Short Circuit = Negative Emotion

Straighten out the short circuit and the negative emotion goes away and, with it, the illness, blocks or barriers that are inhibiting you.

Simply put, energy flows around the body like a river, but that energy can get blocked, in the same way as a log can block a river. The energy cannot continue to flow until the blockage is removed. It will either build up or take an alternate course. This can cause a 'short circuit' in the energy system that needs to be corrected.

To correct it, all you need to do is tap the meridian at a specified point while focusing on the problem.

Right now, you are probably thinking, 'Come off it, it cannot be that simple.' But I will prove it to you. You do not even have to believe it, it will work anyway. The technique takes 10 minutes to learn.

Your Daily Affirmation

Now is the time to choose a daily affirmation. Make no mistake; affirmations used properly are your most powerful tool to self-improvement. However, the critical factor is actually choosing a suitable affirmation. Here are a few examples:

- *I am relaxed and confident when taking my Practical Test.*
- *I can take my Practical Test with confidence.*
- *I am calm and confident when taking my Practical Test.*

As the use of your affirmation will be dominant in your preparation, when choosing your affirmation you must bear three things in mind:

1: The affirmation must be in the present tense, as if you are taking your test now.

2: It must also relate to taking your test, and not passing. This is because you will not know if you pass until the end of your test, so you need to take it to pass. If you are 'calm and confident when passing your test', your unconscious mind may think that this means you will be calm and confident when you are being told that you have passed. Your unconscious mind can take things very literally!

3: You need to choose an affirmation that gets you going. One that makes you say 'Yeah' when you repeat it, one that appeals to all of your hopes, dreams and desires.

There is truth in the old saying 'Beware of what you wish for, it may just come true'.

For the purpose of this section, I will use 'I am relaxed and confident when taking my Practical Test', but you can simply substitute this for an affirmation that is more appropriate for you.

Do you remember at the beginning of the Practical Test section I asked you to score this statement?

Wouldn't it be nice to be able to increase that score?

Well, that is exactly what we are going to do.

Chapter 6
THE PROCESS

At first, the steps may appear long-winded or cumbersome, but as you become acquainted with them, a complete round will only take about a minute or less.

The technique consists of four stages and is known as the EFT sandwich.

1. **The Setup**
2. **The Sequence** (bread)
3. **The Gamut Procedure** (cheese)
4. **The Sequence Repeated** (bread)

As mentioned earlier, you will need to focus in on the problem while tapping the specific points listed in **The Sequence** section. When going through this process, it is best to keep the following guidelines in mind.

• If any of the points feel nicer than others, it may be

worthwhile tapping these a little longer, for as long as you want; in fact, you cannot overtap.

- If any point feels sore or really hurts, try switching to the other side of the body, or just touching the point for two breaths without tapping.

- Your body may react in different ways so do not be alarmed if something out of the ordinary happens. You may be opening meridians that have not flowed properly for some time, and that can feel strange.

- After doing this procedure for the first time, I would recommend that you give yourself two or three days before trying it again. This will give your body time to settle.

1: The Setup

To achieve success, you need to prepare your unconscious mind, and that includes neutralising blocks to healing. This is done in The Setup.

Decide which hand you would feel most comfortable tapping with – if you are right-handed, this will probably be your right hand, and vice versa.

Now look at your non-tapping hand palm upwards. Locate the edge of your hand in-between the wrist and base of your little finger. This is the point where you would 'karate chop' something if you so desired! It is therefore called the Karate Chop or KC point (see the diagram on page 156).

Remind yourself of your affirmation

Say out loud the following statements while tapping the KC point on one hand with the four fingers of the other hand.

- 'Even though *it will never be possible* for me to achieve my goal statement, I want to deeply and completely accept myself.'

- 'Even though *it is unsafe* for me to achieve my goal statement, I want to deeply and completely accept myself.'

- 'Even though *it is unsafe for others* for me to achieve my goal statement, I want to deeply and completely accept myself.'

- 'Even though *I have unique blocks stopping me* from achieving my goal statement, I want to deeply and completely accept myself.'

- 'Even though *I don't deserve* to achieve my goal statement, I want to deeply and completely accept myself.'

As you said those statements, did any of them touch a nerve, or 'hit the spot'?

If so, write the statement here:

✎

Is there anything that you think that you ought to have said? Yes/No

If so, write it here:

(The Setup statement should begin **'Even though I ...'** and finish with **'... I want to deeply and completely accept myself.'**)

✎ *Even though I have unique blocks stopping me for ... achieving my goal. Statement I want to deeply & completely accept myself ... I will pass my driving test*

If you have written any further statements, then say these three times each while tapping the KC point with the four fingers of the other hand.

2: The Sequence

- - - - - - - - - - - - - -

The following diagrams show the points that you need to tap. It does not matter what side of the body you use, or indeed if you switch sides while in the middle of the sequence. Tapping should be done fairly firmly but not enough to bruise yourself! If a point hurts, instead of tapping just hold the point for two breaths. If you physically cannot tap a point, then don't worry, you could imagine tapping it or miss it out altogether. You should tap about seven times fairly quickly.

| EB
Eyebrow | At beginning of
eyebrow at top of nose | Use the index finger and
middle finger to tap this point |

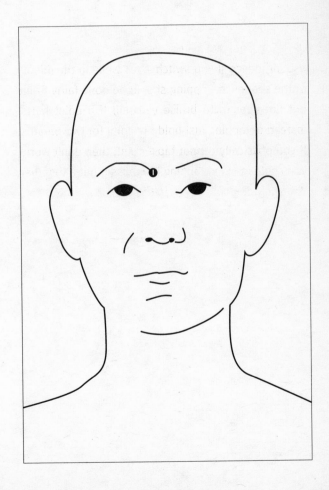

EC Eye Corner	On bone on outside corner of eye	Use the index finger and middle finger to tap this point

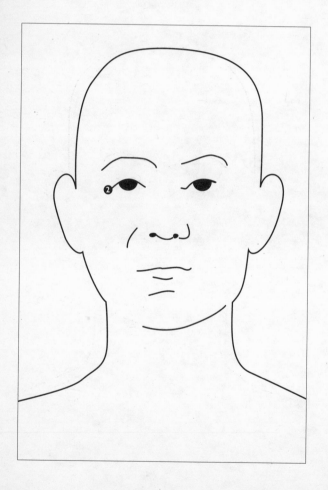

UE **Under** **Eye**	On bone just under the eye	Use the index finger and middle finger to tap this point

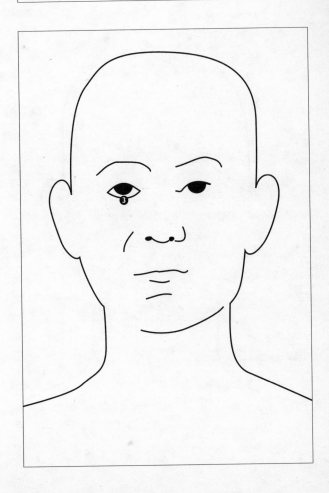

UN Under Nose	Between nose and upper lip	Use the index finger and middle finger to tap this point

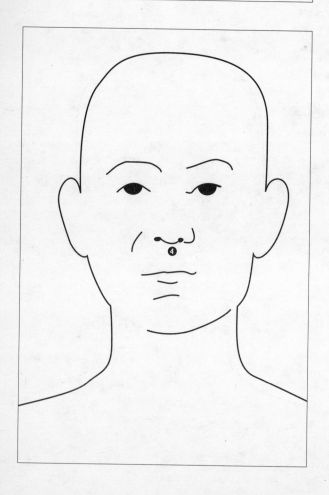

CH **Chin**	Centre of chin under lower lip	Use the index finger and middle finger to tap this point

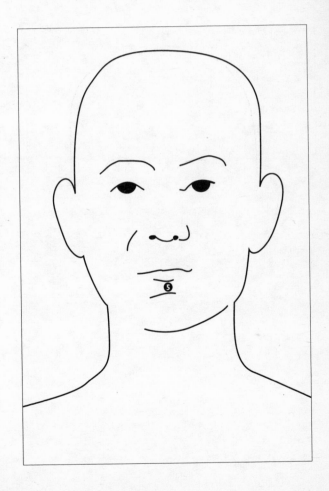

CB Collarbone	Place finger on collarbone. Move it into centre of body until you reach the corner of the collarbone	Use all four fingers to tap the corner of the collarbone hard if you can

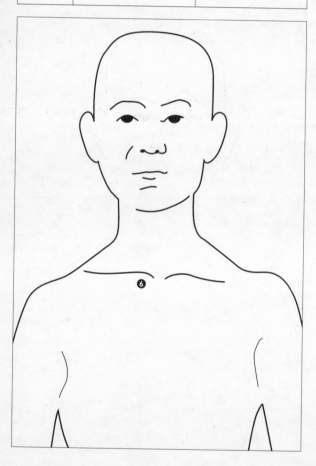

UA Under Arm	Under the arm approx. 4ins below armpit in line with the nipple	Use a flat palm to 'lightly slap' this point

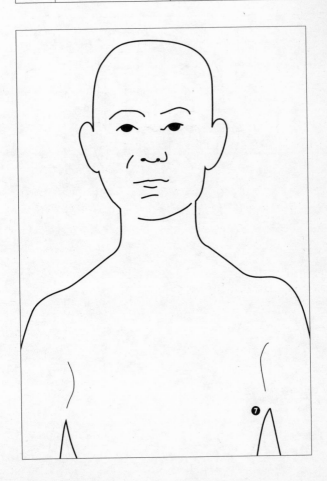

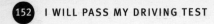

TH Thumb	Outside edge of thumb at base of nail	Use the index finger and middle finger to tap this point

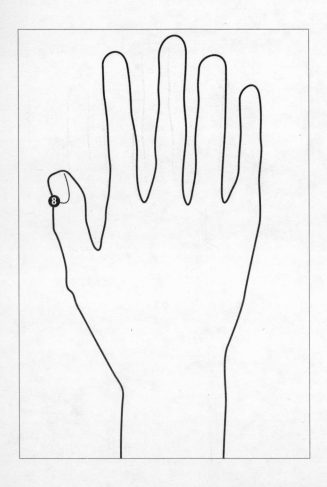

IF Index Finger	At base of nail on side facing thumb	Use the index finger and middle finger to tap this point

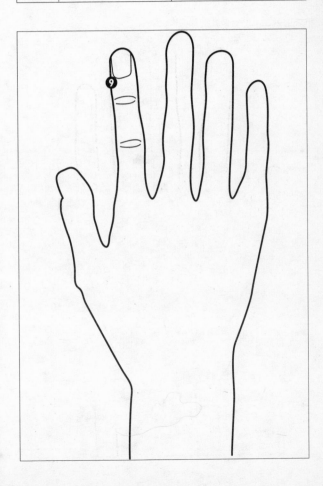

MF Middle Finger	At base of nail on side facing thumb	Use the index finger and middle finger to tap this point

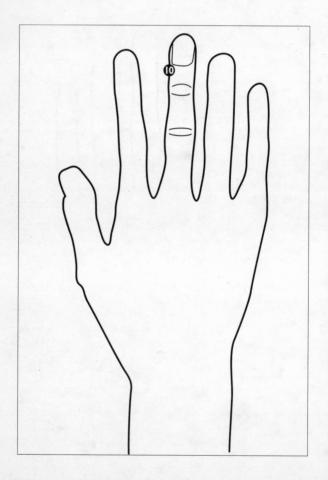

LF Little Finger	At base of nail on side facing thumb	Use the index finger and middle finger to tap this point

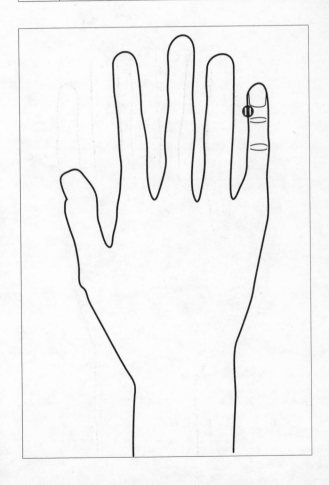

KC **Karate** **Chop**	Outside of hand between top of wrist bone and base of little finger	Use all four fingers to tap this point

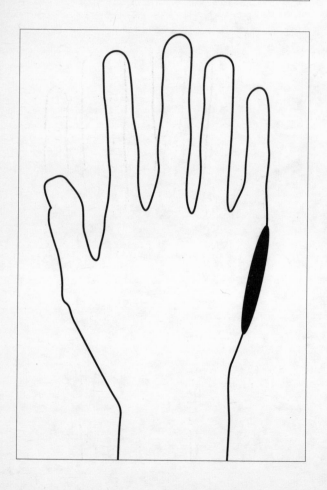

GS Gamut Spot	Back of hand, in-between ring and little finger knuckles, about 1 in back up hand	Use the index finger and middle finger to tap this point

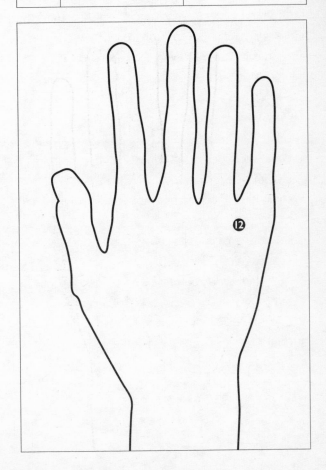

3: The Gamut Procedure

While you continually tap the Gamut Point, perform the following steps. These steps will fine tune the brain and help the brain to become more balanced. This looks probably even more strange than the earlier steps!

1. Close your eyes
2. Open your eyes
3. Look hard down left while holding your head straight
4. Look hard down right while holding your head straight
5. Roll your eyes in a **steady** circle, as if your nose was the centre of a clock
6. Roll your eyes in a **steady** circle in the opposite direction
7. Count rapidly from 1 to 5
8. Hum a few notes of a tune
9. Count rapidly from 1 to 5

4: The Sequence Repeated

Now repeat **The Sequence**, working through all the individual treatment points, from The Eyebrow to The Gamut Spot.

That is the end of this part of the technique. So how have you done? Repeat out loud your affirmation.

'Taking my Theory Test is fun, easy and enjoyable.'

Now score your belief in your ability to achieve this.

✎

No Belief 0 1 2 3 4 5 6 7 8 9 10 **Absolute Belief**

Has it increased? If so, by how much?

Repeat the steps above, but you will not need to do **The Gamut Procedure** again, until you get your score as high as possible.

In the unlikely event of your score not increasing try changing rooms, and drinking water before trying again. (See the **Troubleshooting** section on page 188.)

Daily affirmation: *'Taking my Theory Test is fun, easy and enjoyable.'*

This is your daily affirmation. Make no mistake, this is one of your most useful tools to passing your Theory Test. You should start to say this every day as soon as possible. It does not matter if you believe it or not; you could use EFT to boost your belief daily, but if not, just saying it every day, whether you believe it or not, will have a powerfully positive effect on you. If you find yourself thinking 'But ...' then neutralise the 'but' by using EFT.

For example, you could say to yourself, 'Taking my Theory Test is fun, easy and enjoyable,' but into your mind pops '... but you are a failure' or '... but you are not ready'. These are the thoughts to eliminate as they serve no useful purpose. .

I will now show you just how to eliminate all of those negative thoughts and emotions.

Chapter 7
CLEARING THE BLOCKS

- - - - - - - - - - - - - -

Now that your belief in your affirmation has improved, you need to start breaking down your blocks to success. These are the blocks that you listed earlier in Chapter 4.

This is done using the four stages outlined in Chapter 6.

1. **The Setup**
2. **The Sequence**
3. **The Gamut Procedure**
4. **The Sequence Repeated**

Turn back to the list of blocks that you wrote down earlier and select one to erase now. For the purpose of this exercise, I will use '*I have failed before therefore I will probably fail again*'.

Now score your belief in your statement:

No Belief 0 1 2 3 4 5 6 7 8 9 10 Absolute Belief

Your aim now is to get the score as low as possible.

1: The Setup
Tapping the KC spot repeat:

> 'Even though *I have failed before and will probably fail again*, I want to deeply and completely accept myself.'

Yours may be:
> 'Even though *my nerves affect me*, I want to deeply and completely accept myself.'

or
> 'Even though *I am not confident enough*, I want to deeply and completely accept myself.'

2: The Sequence
Now choose a reminder statement to say as you tap on each point. I am going to say '**I will probably fail again**'.

Now tap on all of the treatment points while repeating your reminder statement. Really tune into and think about your block.

Remember:

- If any of the points feel nicer than others, it may be worthwhile tapping these a little longer, for as long as you want, in fact; you cannot overtap

- If any point feels sore or really hurts, try switching to the other side of the body, or just holding the point for two breaths

- Your body may react in different ways, so do not be alarmed if something out of the ordinary happens. You may be opening meridians that have not flowed properly for some time, and that can feel strange

3: The Gamut Procedure

Now perform The Gamut Procedure as described in Chapter 6 on page 158.

4: The Sequence Repeated

Repeat the sequence.

Now score your belief in your block:

No Belief 0 1 2 3 4 5 6 7 8 9 10 Absolute Belief

Has it gone down? Do the whole treatment again, *although you need not do The Gamut Procedure again*, until you get your score as low as you possibly can.

Now repeat this process for each of your blocks. I realise that this may take a little time, but you are eradicating a lifetime's worth of blocks and replacing them with one – your affirmation.

If, like many of us, you have a great long list that keeps growing as you identify more blocks, then just do two, three or as many as you can cope with, each day. You will notice that as you eradicate them one by one, you will start to feel better in yourself, your confidence may improve and you may begin to feel more relaxed.

When you are happy that you have cleared these blocks, then please proceed.

Finding a Booster Spot

It would be very useful if you could identify one or two specific points that really work for you. This would be an important find, as it may provide a shortcut for you; instead of tapping all of the points in sequence, just tap the ones that make a difference. This will cut out all of the other stages.

When you are in a stressful situation and want to relax, if you have found a booster spot that helps you relax, then that is all you will need to tap. In fact, if you are in a public place and you wish to be discreet, you will not even have to tap; you can just touch the point while you are breathing. All you need to do is think of a problem, give it a name for your reminder statement, score it, and then just tap your booster spot.

When going through **The Sequence**, are there any particular points that feel really nice for you? Why not try scoring your belief after each point and seeing if any has a positive effect on your score? A booster spot may be specific to a particular problem; for instance, a spot that helps you to relax may be different from one that increases your confidence. It is just a matter of finding the ones that work for you.

Chapter 8

VISUALISATION – TAKING THE TEST IN YOUR MIND

- - - - - - - - - - - - - - - - -

You may well want to forget it, but your test will not go away! An effective tool available for your use at any time is to take the test in your mind. This will work for both the Practical and Theory Tests. This is not as weird as it may sound. If you doubt the effectiveness of this exercise, cast your mind back to the earlier chapter when I explained about the unconscious mind. It does not reason or think, it just obeys. More importantly, it cannot tell the difference between you visualising or imagining something and reality. The more real it seems in your mind, the more effective it will be.

In your mind, go into the waiting room and sit down. It does not matter if you have never been in there; just imagine what it may be like. What does it feel like? Are you nervous, anxious ... are you getting any feeling at all?

I would imagine that most of us would be nervous. If just thinking about it does not raise any emotion, but you know that it will be there on the day, then try again, but really try to imagine it. What does the room look like in your mind, what does it smell like, is there a pile of magazines on the table? Imagine your name being called out and you have to go forward to take the test. You are now in your car about to commence the test. Now score the feeling from 0 to 10 on the scale below.

No Feeling 0 1 2 3 4 5 6 7 8 9 10 **Extreme Feeling**

Give it a name – *nervousness*, *anxiety*, etc. (This will be your reminder statement.)

Now do the technique to neutralise that feeling, while thinking about the situation. You will need to treat each emotion separately. Do as many rounds as it takes to bring the emotional intensity down to as low a score as possible.

Your statement may be:

'Even though I am nervous when taking my test, I deeply and completely accept myself.'

Now imagine going out to the car and beginning your driving test. As you go through it in your mind, as soon as you start to feel any emotional content from each situation then perform the following steps:

- Score the feeling
- Give it a name (this will be your reminder statement)
- Now use EFT to neutralise the feeling

Rerun the situation in your mind; if there is no emotional content, then you can proceed with your Practical Test.

Why not try the set-pieces in your mind as well?

Take the whole test in your mind. Treat the emotional content of each situation using the four steps above. When you can take the test competently in your mind, then you are a significant step closer to passing.

Make no mistake about it. Using the visualisation technique will significantly improve your chances of passing if performed correctly.

Specific Blocks

For many of us, one particular part of the test will cause the most problems, the most nerves and a greater chance of not passing.

Why not use EFT to help with that specific situation?

Let's use an example: *'I cannot reverse.'*

Use EFT to overcome this and move on to any other specific fears.

Score how much you hate computers. (o would be no hate, while 10 would be absolute hatred.) Follow the simple steps, and why not look for a booster spot?

Start off with T**he Setup**: *'Even though I cannot reverse, I deeply and completely accept myself.'*

Next, do **The Sequence**, your reminder statement could be simply *'I cannot reverse,'* while you think about reversing and how much you dislike it.

Next do **The Gamut Procedure**.
Now do **The Sequence Repeated**.

Now score *I cannot reverse*. Has it gone down? It should have. If not, see the **Troubleshooting** section on page 188.

Now repeat the process until you get the score as low as possible; you should be able to get it down to a o or 1. You need not perform **The Gamut Procedure** again.

Perform these stages for any specific problems, fears or anxieties that you have.

Score your belief that you will pass your Practical Test.

Confidence Booster

You can also use EFT to help increase your confidence.

Let's use *'I believe that I can pass my Practical Test.'*

No Belief o 1 2 3 4 5 6 7 8 9 10 Absolute Belief

What is your score? If it is low then you can perform the four stages of EFT to help in this area. Follow the simple steps; it would be extremely beneficial to find a booster spot for this exercise, and I have written out the steps below with this in mind. Remember, you are looking for individual points that substantially increase your score, or perhaps just feel different.

Start off with **The Setup**: *'Even though I don't believe that I can pass my Practical Test, I deeply and completely accept myself.'* Now score the statement.

No Belief 0 1 2 3 4 5 6 7 8 9 10 **Absolute Belief**

Next, do **The Sequence**. Your reminder statement could be simply '*I don't believe*', while you think about taking the test and how much you don't believe that you can pass. After you tap each individual point, score your statement.

Next do **The Gamut Procedure**.

Now do **The Sequence Repeated**.

Score the statement again. Try just tapping the booster spot while repeating '*disbelief*', and see if it makes a difference. If not, you have got the wrong spot, or you need to do the complete procedure again. Now score '*I believe that I can pass my Practical Test.*' Has it gone up? It should have. If not, see the **Troubleshooting** section on page 188.

Relaxation

You may also benefit from two techniques for relaxation. The first one is possibly the most effective relaxation technique that I know. It works really well, especially if you are very stressed. Here is what you do:

Method 1

- Sit comfortably (you may lie down if you wish, but I find sitting is the best position)
- Cross your legs
- Cross your arms over in the opposite direction. Let them rest loosely in your lap
- Breathe in through your nose with the tip of your tongue on the roof of your mouth (this is to connect two meridians – the Central Meridian and the Governing Meridian)
- Breathe out through your mouth with your tongue down flat. As you exhale, repeat 'balance'
- As you exhale and repeat 'balance', let your body relax further with each breath. Personally, I concentrate on letting my shoulders relax and the rest of my body seems to follow
- Do this for two minutes

> **Note: This is a powerful technique so do not overdo it, especially if you are about to drive or operate heavy machinery.**

Method 2

If you are feeling especially tense, then EFT is a useful tool. I have written it down below, again with the intention of finding a booster spot. If you have already found a booster spot, then just try tapping that point alone while repeating *'tension'*. If this does not work, then you will have to find another booster spot for 'tension' or go through the complete procedure:

- Score how tense you feel (0 being completely relaxed while 10 is very tense)
- Start off with **The Setup**. *'Even though I am tense, I deeply and completely accept myself'*
- Now score the statement

Next, do **The Sequence**. Your reminder statement could be simply 'this tension', while you think about sitting the test and how much you don't believe that you can pass. After you tap each individual point, score your statement.

✎

Next do **The Gamut Procedure**.

Now do **The Sequence Repeated**.

✎

Score the statement again. Try just tapping the booster spot while repeating 'this tension', and see if it makes a difference. If not, you have got the wrong spot, or you need to do the complete procedure again. So the day of your Practical Test is here. From the very moment you wake up, you should be thinking, 'I am relaxed and confident when taking my Practical Test,' or your chosen affirmation.

On the Day

Use EFT to eliminate any last-minute worries and nerves. Practise the relaxation technique, and do not allow any negative thoughts about passing your Practical Test to pop into your head. If they do, simply dismiss them and replace with your affirmation.

Dress to feel good. Wear clothes that make you feel special.

Arrive in good time.

When waiting, use the booster spot if necessary. As I mentioned before, all you need to do is hold the point concerned. You may also practise the relaxation technique unobtrusively in the waiting room. Believe me, I have done it, and people are normally too wrapped up in their own concerns to worry about you. If you wish to do a last-minute round of EFT, then perhaps you could dash to the loo!

If you feel that you would like to try other simple and discreet methods of controlling your nerves, providing you with more focus, or a feeling of confidence and control, refer to the Breathing Exercises section on page 178. You will find three different exercises which can be practised well in advance of your tests, and then you can use them just before the test itself to provide you with an extra tool to achieve success.

It may also be useful to remind yourself of the practical advice provided in the Practical Tips section in Chapter 3.

Good luck!

PART 4

USEFUL
INFORMATION

- - - - - - - - - - -

BREATHING EXERCISES

These exercises are a useful tool to aid the meridian flow, relax and invigorate. The **Collarbone Breathing** exercise will help you if you are having trouble shifting your score to any significant degree. You should not need this but, if you do, then perform this routine before you start your treatment. The **Balanced Breathing** and **Calming Breath** exercises are relaxation techniques that you could easily utilise in a quiet moment before your test.

Collarbone Breathing

This technique utilises 40 breathing and tapping movements. During the exercise, keep your arms away from your body so that only your fingertips and knuckles touch your body.

1. Place two fingers of your right hand on your right collarbone point, and with two fingers of your left hand tap the gamut point on your right hand continuously while you:

2. Breathe in halfway and hold for seven taps

3. Breathe all the way in and hold for seven taps

4. Breathe out halfway and hold for seven taps

5. Breathe all the way out and hold for seven taps

6. Breathe normally for seven taps

7. Now place the two fingers from your right hand on your left collarbone and repeat

8. Next, bend the fingers on your right hand and place the knuckles on your right collarbone and repeat

9. Now place the knuckles of your right hand on your left collarbone and repeat

10. You have now done half the procedure; do the same routine as in points 1–6 above, but this time using the left hand to touch the collarbone

Balanced Breathing

This is a wonderful exercise, especially if you are feeling particularly stressed or 'unbalanced'. To my mind, it is the best breathing exercise bar none.

1. Sit upright in a chair

2. Cross your feet over

3. Cross your arms over in the opposite direction to your feet

4. Turn palms in towards each other and hold hands (your wrists should be crossed)

5. Breathe in through your nose with the tip of your

tongue on the roof of your mouth (this ensures that two powerful channels, the Central and Governing vessels, are connected)

6. Breathe out through your mouth with your tongue lying flat. As you breathe out, think 'balance'

7. Continue for two minutes only

Diaphragmatic Breathing –
The Calming Breath

Breathing solely from the diaphragm needs practice. You need to spend a few minutes each day for one week until you are able to use this method while sitting, lying, standing or walking. As soon as you start to feel any stress or anxiety, begin to use the diaphragmatic breathing; this will immediately have a calming effect and will, in most instances, avert the anxiety and stress. It is no use waiting until the stress reaches its height; it needs to be practised at the beginning to prevent the stress from building and becoming unmanageable.

1. Place the flat of your right hand on your diaphragm (the top of your stomach), left hand on chest

2. Looking down, begin by taking a 'normal' breath in and, as you do so, notice the movement of your hands as you breathe in and out

3. Now, taking another breath in, physically push out the diaphragm, making sure that the left hand – on the chest – does not move; you are only concerned with the movement of the diaphragm

4. As you breathe out, you should feel your right hand return to its original position

5. Repeat

If you find **Diaphragmatic Breathing** difficult, here are a couple of ideas that may help you.

• Imagine that you have a piece of string, about 10ins long, coming out of your diaphragm. Now imagine holding that piece of string about 10ins away from your body; begin moving that string away from your body very, very slowly while you take a slow, deep breath in through your nose. And, as you are breathing in, allow your diaphragm to come out with that string. After counting for 'three elephants' (as in 'one elephant, two elephants, three elephants ...') – slowly let that piece of string gently move back towards your body, letting the string hang loosely, and you'll find that you are releasing that 'calming' breath from your body nice and slowly while you are letting the string return back to its loose position.

• Try this breathing exercise using a straw. Breathe in and out through the straw.

Initially, watch yourself in front of a mirror. If the left hand (on the chest) moves, you are doing it incorrectly. It is then easier to practise while lying down and I suggest that you practise for a few minutes when you wake up in the morning and a few minutes before going to sleep at night.

At first, you will probably find that it is only possible to take two or three diaphragmatic breaths before needing to gasp and maybe take a few deep breaths. Don't worry, this is quite normal and you will find that, with practice, you will be able to breathe diaphragmatically for a few minutes at a time.

Many people practise this form of breathing for a couple of days and think that is all they need to do. It does need practice so that it can be called upon to be used automatically and efficiently as and when needed.

If you experience any discomfort or dizziness, stop immediately and ask an expert for help, as you might not be doing the breathing correctly.

THE MERIDIANS, POINTS AND HOW THEY AFFECT YOU

Meridian	Point	When Blocked	When Tapped	Psychological	Physical
Bladder	EB	Increase of fear and intimidation	Increases courage and releases fear	Courage, energy, fear, free expression, forgetfulness, frustration, impatience, inhibition, lethargy, restlessness, short-term memory recall, trauma, thinking processes	Automatic nervous system, lower back pain, bones, ears, hair loss, head, incontinence, osteoporosis, parasympathetic nervous system, prostate, spinal column, sympathetic nervous system, teeth, urinatory system, vertigo
Gall Bladder	EC	Depletes energy	Increases determination, and removes lethargy	Calm, courage, determination, indecision, clarity of mind	Lack of bile, fat digestion, eye problems, lack of flexibility, gall bladder, gall stones, headaches, indigestion, stiff joints, painful joints, migraine, stiff/painful muscles, poor stamina, stiff neck, stiffness, tendons/ ligaments

Eye brow

Eye corner

Meridian	Point	When Blocked	When Tapped	Psychological	Physical
Stomach	UE	Muddled thinking	Releases indecisive emotions and helps thinking process	Addictions, anxiety, confused thought, deprivation, disorientation, dogmatic thinking, harmony, indecisiveness, intuition, obsessiveness	Appetite disorders, anorexia nervosa, breasts, chewing mouth and lips, upper digestive passages, endometriosis, fibroids, flesh, hiatus hernia, indigestion, mastitis, menstrual problems, nausea, ovaries, prolapses, sickness, sleep cycles, stomach, vomiting, weight problems
Governing	UN	Introvertedness	Removes shyness and helps communication skills	Communication, embarrassment, introvertedness, panic, relationships, sex problems, shyness, worry	Backache, nasal congestion, epilepsy, nerves, sexual disorders, tremors, vitality
Conception/ Central	CH	Holds past traumatic events	Releases pre-birth and birth trauma, and allows energy to circulate	Birth and pre-birth trauma, fatigue, indecision, panic, shame, trauma, worry	Abdomen, backache, chest, coldness, face, fibroids, hernia, lumps, lungs, menopause, nerves, reproductive problems, throat, weakness

Meridian	Point	When Blocked	When Tapped	Psychological	Physical
Kidney	CB	Low energy, poor decision-making	Helps willpower and impetus to carry out tasks	Gentleness, willpower, impetus to carry out tasks	Ageing, accident proneness, backache, balance problems, bones, chronic tiredness, congenital diseases, developmental irregularities, hereditary diseases, ears, endocrine imbalances, energy level for activity, exhaustion, genetic inheritance, hearing problems, hormonal imbalances, kidneys, osteoporosis, physical development, puberty, reproductive problems, sexual activity, stumbling, teeth, vertigo, weakness
Spleen	UA	Slows down thinking	Increases concentration and improved thinking patterns	Addictions, anxiety, decision-making	Anaemia, appetite, over-eating, bleeding disorders, diabetes, food digestion, digestive enzymes, hypoglycemia, periods, weight problems
Lung	TH	Lethargy and low energy	Releases negativity and increases positivity and vitality	Courage, disdain, intolerance, obsessive compulsive disorder, righteousness	Asthma, breathing disorders, tightness in chest, coughing, dry skin, eczema, emphysema, lungs, nasal congestion, nose, spots

Meridian	Point	When Blocked	When Tapped	Psychological	Physical
Large Intestine	IF	Nostalgia and harking for past	Releases emotions and causes us to live in the past. Increases goal-setting skills and optimism	Guilt, living in the past, wellbeing	Bowels, catarrh, constipation, diarrhoea, digestion, diverticulitis, irritable bowel syndrome, intestinal problems, mucus, nasal congestion, sinuses, skin
Circulation Sex	MF	Low self-esteem	Increases willpower and releases inferiority	Advancing, humour, jealousy, regret, sex problems, unhappiness, willpower	Hardening of arteries, angina, blood pressure, tightness of chest, circulation, heart disease, inhalant-type allergies, palpitations, sex problems, veins
Heart	LF	Chest pains, loneliness and selfishness	Develops empathy, compassion and unconditional love. Removes limited thinking	Compassion, consciousness, empathy, joy, unconditional love	Central nervous system, circulation, heart disease, night sweats, speech disorders, sweat glands, tongue
Small Intestine	KC	Lack of confidence, self-hate	Removes self-doubt, feelings of low self-esteem and improves confidence	Anxiety, cloudy judgement, lack of confidence, decision-making, doubt, self-hate, low self-esteem, mind clarity, shock, sadness, self-doubt, thinking processes	Abdominal pain, anaemia, circulation, gas, nutrient absorption, small intestine
Triple Warmer	GS	Inability to express love and emotions	Opens us to emotional interaction with others	Emotional coldness, communication, depression, low self-esteem, loneliness, living in the past, past problems, repressed emotions, resentment, self-hate, unsociability	Allergies, bladder, chilliness, fluid retention, heat regulation, immune system, infections (low resistance, intestinal problems) separation and evacuation, kidneys, liver, breathing, lymphatic system, physical pain, toxins, spleen, stomach

TROUBLESHOOTING

My score will not go down

Are you tapping for the right thing? A problem can often have many different faces. The technique WILL work if you are addressing the right thing. If a wheel has fallen off your car and you change the exhaust, the car will still not go.

Sometimes these things take a little perseverance. Do you remember the children's game, where you make a sandcastle and put a coin on top? Each child takes turns in taking a scoop from the sand, and eventually the sand collapses into a pile.

Imagine your problem is the coin, and the scooping is done with EFT. The pile of sand is your emotions connected with the problem. If there is only one emotion (e.g. shame), then the problem will only need one scoop! However, as there are normally many aspects to each problem, you need to treat each of these individually before the coin will drop.

Are you tapping the right points? Check the positioning on the chart entitled **The Meridians, Points and How They Affect You** on page 184.

I have tried all of that and it is still not working

There are such things called 'energy toxins'. These prevent the technique from having its full effect. Unfortunately, they are difficult to trace, but fortunately rare. Try drinking water, changing rooms, changing clothes, sitting in a different chair, etc. The toxin may be in the fabric of the clothes you wear or something you have eaten. Go without tea/coffee three hours before a session and drink plenty of water.

You could also choose to do one of the breathing exercises explained in Part 4. They will help the meridians to flow evenly and in the right direction.

If none of these work, then have a shower without using soaps of any kind and try again. If there is still no result, then the toxin has probably been ingested. Virtually anything can be toxic to your body and therefore interfere with your energy system. The most likely candidates are those things that you eat lots of. Try cutting these out for a couple of days and trying again. The most common items (though they may not be toxic to you) are as follows: perfume, herbs, wheat, corn, refined sugar, coffee, tea, caffeine, alcohol, nicotine, dairy, pepper. Bear in mind that your intuition is often accurate. What do you think it is?

How do I tap?

Tapping should be done fairly firmly but not enough to bruise yourself! If a point hurts, instead of tapping just hold the point for two breaths. If you physically cannot tap a point, then don't worry, you could imagine tapping it or miss it out altogether. You should tap about seven times fairly quickly. My website **www.ilivelifefree.com** has video clips of me tapping all of the points. You are welcome to visit.

Are there any shortcuts?

After you have used the technique for a little while, you may find that you can omit **The Setup** stage and often **The Gamut Procedure** . This will leave you with **The Sequence** and **The Sequence Repeated** . If any points really 'do the trick' for you, i.e. they are really effective, then try using just these. The rule is to try it and see – you can always go back and do the complete technique.

USEFUL CONTACTS AND FURTHER INFORMATION

Websites

Try these websites for more information:

www.learners.co.uk – A useful site with a theory test simulator and a National Directory of Driving Tuition for you to locate driving schools in your area. This facility will also help you look for specific requests, such as disabled facilities.

www.2pass.co.uk – A visually entertaining site with lots of good information and links to a theory test simulator.

www.ilivelifefree.com – my own site. This contains video clips of all of the tapping points

www.emofree.com – Gary Craig's website, packed with information and case histories. Highly Recommended.

www.theamt.com – For Meridian Therapies in the UK.

www.healthypages.co.uk – Good reference point for therapists and seekers.

www.jbennette.com – A therapist in the US; some useful information here, including streaming video of the process.

www.meridian-therapy.com – Association for the
Advancement of Meridian Therapies, listings of
practitioners and training events.

www.energytherapies.org – Chrissie Hardisty is a Director
of the AMT. This site is a good reference point.

Private Treatment

To find an EFT practitioner in your area you may email me at
livelifefree@hotmail.com with your contact details, and I
will put you in touch with your nearest practitioner.
Alternatively, you may telephone free on 0800 083 0796.
This is normally an answerphone service.

OTHER PUBLICATIONS
BY THE AUTHOR

Mind over Weight
Published by Metro, Mind over Weight explores why diets
don't work, the role of the unconscious and the reasons
why many people just cannot lose weight.
ISBN 1 84358 000 4